ETHICAL H4CKING

DARK SIDE OF INTERNET

BINESH MADHARAPU

Contents

Foreword

We exist in a time where hackers hold more influence than ever before. Hacking can now impact the lives of millions of people by targeting elections, power grids, and all sorts of infrastructure that people rely on for their day-to-day activities, not to mention their well-being.

Preface

Ethical hacking strikes all of us as a subject that requires a great deal of prerequisite knowledge about things like heavy duty software, languages that includes hordes of syntaxes, algorithms that could be generated by maestros only. Well that's not the case, to some extent. This book introduces the steps required to complete a penetration test, or ethical hack. Requiring no prior hacking experience, the book explains how to utilize and interpret the results of modern day hacking tools that are required to complete a penetration test. Coverage includes Backtrack Linux, Google Reconnaissance, MetaGooFil, dig, Nmap, Nessus, Metasploit, Fast Track Autopwn, Netcat, and Hacker Defender rootkit. Simple explanations of how to use these tools.

This book is designed for those who just wanted to start their career in Ethical Hacking. I am not going to tell you about social media account Hacking. The goal of this book is to teach everyone the basics of hacking and tell you how to start in this field as a beginner. "ETHICAL H4CKING" Makes the world of hacking more accessible by providing you the roadmap of Ethical Hacking. In our second edition, we will discuss how to perform hacking attacks & how to perform penetration tests!

Acknowledgements

“*“Thanks to everyone .”*”

Table Of Content

ONE
INTRO TO HACKING

Hacking:

Hacking is the process of exploiting system vulnerabilities and compromising security systems to gain unauthorized access to the system resources. It involves a modifying system or application features to achieve a goal outside of the creator's original purpose.

Ethical Hacking:

Ethical Hacking is the process to identify vulnerabilities to assure system security by use of hacking tools, tricks, and techniques. It focuses on simulating methods used by attackers to verify the existence of exploitable vulnerabilities in the system's security.

Hacker:

Hackers are intelligent individuals who spend enormous amounts of time exploring computing resources like networks, websites, mobile devices, etc. to identify critical vulnerabilities which can be used for exploitation.

Ethical Hacker:

Ethical Hacker is an expert in computer internals and networking concepts, who tries to find out potential vulnerabilities on the target systems before a hacker could use, without actually doing any harm to the information systems on behalf of the owners of the IT Assets.

Types of Hackers

Black Hat (Crackers): Individuals utilize computing skills for malicious or destructive activities.

White Hat: Individuals utilizing hacking skills for the defensive purpose.

Gray Hat: Individuals who work both offensively and defensively.

Suicide Hackers: Hackers who aim to shut down the critical infrastructure for a cause and are not worried about facing punishment.

Script Kiddies: An unskilled hacker who compromises the system by running scripts, tools, and software developed by real hackers.

Cyber Terrorists: Individuals with hacking skills, motivated by religious or political beliefs to create fear by large-scale disruption of computer networks.

Hacktivists: Hackers who promote a political agenda by hacking, especially by defacing or disabling websites.

State-sponsoredSponsored: Individuals employed by the government to penetrate and gain confidential information.

Why Ethical Hacking is Necessary

Ethical Hacker needs to think like malicious Hacker. Ethical hacking is necessary to defend against malicious hackers attempts, by anticipating methods they can use to break into a system.

- To fight against cyber crimes.
- To protect information from getting into wrong hands.
- To build a defensive mechanism that avoids hackers from penetrating.
- To test the organization's infrastructure security.

Steps to Perform Ethical Hacking:

- **Reconnaissance**
- **Scanning**
- **Gaining Access**
- **Maintaining Access**
- **Clearing Tracks**

1. Reconnaissance refers to the pre-attack phase where an attacker observes a target before launching an attack. It may include the target organization's clients, employees, operations, network, and systems

2. Scanning is the phase immediately preceding the attack. Here, the attacker uses the details gathered during reconnaissance to identify specific vulnerabilities. An attacker can gather critical network information such as the mapping of systems, routers, and firewalls by using simple tools such as the standard Windows utility Traceroute.

3. Gaining Access In this phase in which real hacking occurs. Attackers use vulnerabilities identified during the reconnaissance and scanning phase to gain access to the target system or network. Attackers gain access to the target system locally, over a LAN, or over the Internet.

4. Maintaining Access of the target machine and remain undetected. Attackers install a backdoor or a Trojan to gain repeat access. They can also install rootkits at the kernel level to gain full administrative access to the target computer. Rootkits are used to gain access at the operating system level,while a Trojan horse gains access at the application level. Both rootkits and Trojans require users to install them locally.

5. Clearing Tracks is for avoiding legal trouble, attackers will overwrite the server, System and application logs to Avoid suspicion and erase all evidence of their actions. Attackers can execute scripts in the Trojan or rootkit to replace the critical system and log files to hide their presence in the system.

Terminology Vulnerability: In simple words, vulnerability is a loophole, Limitation, or weakness that becomes a source for an attacker to enter into the system.

Exploit: It is a software tool designed to take advantage of a flaw (vulnerability) in a system for malicious purposes.

Payload: A payload is an action, or set of operations has to be done on the target, once the exploit successfully launched. It can be any control or Denial of service, etc.

Hack value: Hack value is a notion among the hackers that something is worth doing. Hackers may feel that breaking down robust network security might give them great satisfaction and that it is something they accomplished that not everyone could do.

Zero-day attack: In a 0-day attack, the attacker exploits the vulnerability before the software developer releases the Patch For them.

What is Information Security

Information security, sometimes shortened to **InfoSec**, is the practice of preventing unauthorized access, disclosure, disruption, destruction, modification, inspection, recording or destruction of information.

Information security's primary focus is the balanced protection of the confidentiality, integrity, and availability of data and focuses on efficient policy implementation, organization productivity.

Elements of Information Security

Information Security is a state of well-being of information and infrastructure in which the possibility of theft, tampering, and disruption of information and services is kept low or tolerable.

- Confidentiality
- Authenticity
- Integrity

IP Tracing

The IP address is one of the most critical pieces of information. To attack the target computer, attackers need to identify the IP address of the target computer. Attackers use different techniques to grab the IP address. Sending tracking emails, or SMS, or some malicious links to grab the IP address of the target computer is called as IP Tracing. In other words, extracting user details (like location) based on IP address is known as IP Tracing or IP Lookup.

IP Spoofing

The basic protocol for sending data over the Internet network and many other computer networks is the Internet Protocol (IP). The protocol specifies that each IP packet must have a header which contains (among other things) the IP address of the sender of the packet IP spoofing is the creation of Internet Protocol (IP) packets which have a modified source address in order to either hide the identity of the sender, to impersonate another computer system, or both. It is a technique often used by hackers to invoke attacks against a target device or the surrounding infrastructure.

IP address spoofing involving the use of a trusted IP address to overcome network security measures, such as authentication based on IP addresses. It is frequently used in denial-of-service attacks, where the objective is to flood the target with an overwhelming volume of traffic, and the attacker does not care about receiving responses to the attack packets.

VPN

A virtual private network (VPN) is allows you to create a secure encrypted connection over a less secure network, such as the public internet to another network. A VPN uses tunneling protocols to encrypt data at the sending end and decrypt it at the receiving end. To provide additional security, the originating and receiving network addresses are also encrypted. The encrypted connection helps ensure that sensitive data is safely transmitted. It prevents unauthorized people from eavesdropping on the traffic and allows the user to conduct work remotely. A VPN is created by establishing a virtual point-to-point connection through the use of dedicated circuits or with tunneling protocols over existing networks.

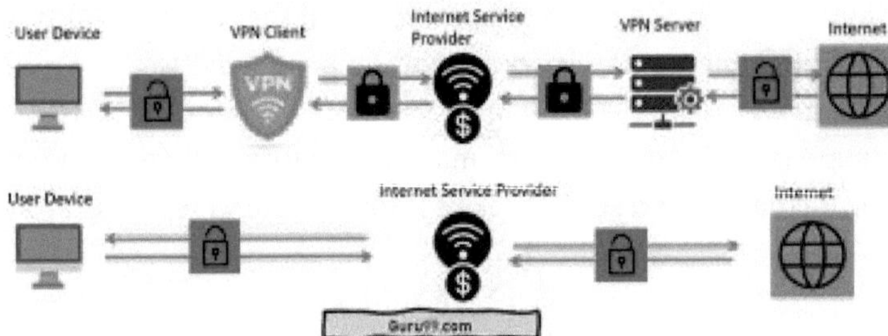

VPS

A VPS is a server created using software virtualization. It functions like a physical server, but it is a virtualized instance created within a server. A single physical machine can host multiple virtual private servers. A cloud-based VPS may be hosted across multiple servers. A VPS runs its own copy of an operating system (OS), and customers may have superuser-level access to that operating system instance, so they can install almost any software that runs on that OS. The technology behind VPS hosting is similar to that of VMware or Virtual Box. These programs allow you to run several virtualized operating systems on one machine.

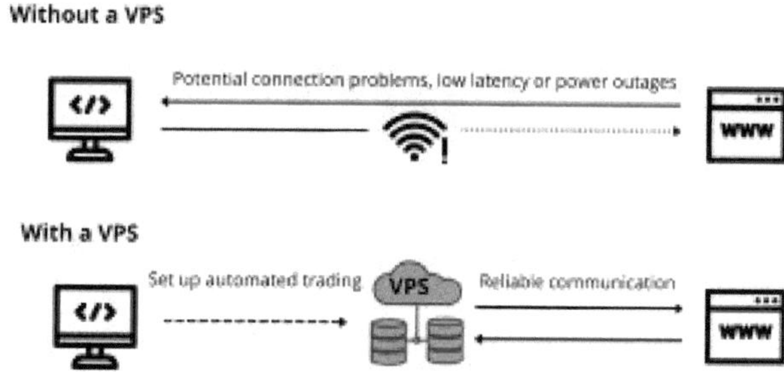

Proxy

A proxy server acts as a gateway between the device and the internet. It's an intermediary server separating end users from the websites they browse. A proxy server thus functions on behalf of the client when requesting service, potentially masking the true origin of the request to the resource server. Proxy servers provide varying levels of functionality, security, and privacy depending on company policy. If a person using a proxy server, internet traffic flows through the proxy server on its way to the requested address. The request then comes back through that same proxy server, and then the proxy server forwards the data received from the website to the requested device. This serves as a method to simplify or control the complexity of the request or provide additional benefits such as load balancing, privacy, or security.

TWO

FOOTPRINTING AND RCONNAISSANCE

Footprinting:

Footprinting is the process of collecting information related to the target network. Footprinting helps in identifying Various ways to intrude into an Organization's network system.

In this step attacker tries to gather publicly available sensitive information, using which he/she can carry out social engineering, perform system or network level attacks, that can cause substantial financial loss or damage the reputation of an individual or organization. This step helps an attacker in gaining a basic idea of network structure and organization's infrastructure details.

Why we perform Footprinting ?

- Footprinting is the first step of the attacking process. Hackers use to gather information about the target environment, usually to find ways to break into that environment.
- Footprinting allows an attacker to know about the security posture of an organization.
- It helps in reducing attacker's attack surface to a specific range of IP address, networks, domain name, remote access, etc.
- It allows an attacker to build their information database about the target's organization security weakness and plan attacks accordingly.

Terminology

Passive Information Gathering: Is the process of collecting information about the target from the publicly accessible resources.

Active Information Gathering: Is the process of gather information about the target by using techniques likes social engineering, grabbing information by visiting personal blogs or websites, or through direct interaction with the individual or employees of the organization.

What kind of information is needed?

Network Information: Domain name, Network blocks, IP address of computers in the target network, TCP and UDP services running, details related to IDS running.

System Information: User and group names, system banners, routing tables information, system architecture, remote system names.

Organization Information: Employee details, organization website details, location details, address and phone numbers, information related to security policies implemented, and any non-technical information about the organization.

How to perform Footprinting?

- Through search engines
- Through social networking sites
- Through official websites
- Direct communication with the target
- Through job portals
- Through DNS enumeration

Google Hacking

Google is a vast resource where millions of pages are available for an average user to search. But getting useful information out of those results is a challenging task, to extract the desired information (information that is useful to attack target individual or network) we can take help of Google search operators also known as google dorks. This technique is called Google Hacking.

By using these google dorks, we query Google to reveal sensitive data, useful for the reconnaissance stage of an attack, sensitive data such as emails associated with an individual or an organization, database files with usernames and passwords, unprotected directories with confidential documents, URLs to login portals, different types of system logs such as firewall and access logs etc.,

whois lookup

While purchasing a domain, the user (registrant) has to provide their contact details, like address, phone number, email id, etc., those registration details along with domain validity information is usually stored in a publicly available database called whois database.

Domain registrars will protect this information from not to be published on the internet based on the request made by users, at extra cost. Domain registration details will not be available on the internet if they opt domain privacy, of course, domain registrar information will be available, whoever wants to get that domain information should contact the registrar, and if the registrar finds the query is legitimate, they will provide the Domain registrant details. By using the free online and offline tools, we extract domain registrant Information from publicly available Whois database. This process is known as whois lookup.

Traceroute

While the data packet is in transit, it passes through multiple network nodes to reach the destination. If the data packet fails to reach the destination, the user will not know the reason behind the failure; network administrators use traceroute program to trace the packet from source to destination to identify the actual cause of the problem so that they can investigate and resolve the issue. Traceroute tool is used to extract details about the path that a packet takes from the source to a specific destination.

Domain

A domain name is an identification string that defines a group of computers that can be accessed and administered with a common set of rules and procedures. Within the Internet, domains are defined by the IP address. All devices sharing a common part of the IP address are said to be in the same domain.

In general, a domain name identifies a network domain, or it represents an Internet Protocol (IP) resource, such as a personal computer used to access the Internet, a server computer hosting a web site, or the web site itself or any other service communicated via the Internet. Domains are formed by the rules and procedures of the Domain Name System (DNS). Any name registered in the DNS is a domain name.

Subdomain

In the Domain Name System (DNS) hierarchy, a subdomain is a domain that is a part of another (main) domain. Subdomains are created to organize and navigate to different sections of your website. You can create multiple subdomains or child domains on your main domain.

The most common use of a subdomain is for creating a testing or staging version of a website. Often developers will test new plugins and updates on a subdomain before publishing them live on the Internet. Another common use of a subdomain is to create an online eCommerce store. Often companies want a separate subdomain to handle transactions because eCommerce sites typically require a more complex set up.

What if We Skip Footprinting?

We should not skip Footprinting. Hacker or penetration tester's success will not always depend on sophisticated tools used to perform attacks, but information gathered at Footprinting plays a crucial role in gaining access to the target.

Want to know how?

Scenario: Information gathered in this step can help us bypass some security controls for example login credentials for one of the computers in the network may be DOB or first name of the employee. As we know some necessary information about an employee, we can try to guess the username or password by observing hint.

Conclusion: launching attacks without proper knowledge about the target may affect the success of the attack.

Countermeasures

- Revise the information before publishing on blogs, social networking sites, and websites.
- Never upload highly classified documents online.
- Privatize the who is lookup registration details by applying for anonymous registration with the web hosting service provider.
- Never click the link in emails or mobiles, if received from an unknown sender.
- Use pseudo-names in blogs and social networking sites to not leak personal information.
- Avoid opening third-party social networking sites or websites from office premises.
- Use IDS in corporate networks to detect Footprinting attacks done by hackers.

Domain Name Information

You can use http://www.whois.com/whois website to get detailed information about a domain name information including its owner, its registrar, date of registration, expiry, name server, owner's contact information, etc.

Finding IP Address

You can use ping command at your prompt. This command is available on Windows as well as on Linux OS. ex: Ping <domainname>

Finding Hosting Company

Once you have the website address, you can get further detail by using ip2location.com website. Following is the example to find out the details of an IP address –

History of the Website

It is very easy to get a complete history of any website using www.archive.org.

You can enter a domain name in the search box to find out how the website was looking at a given point of time and what were the pages available on the website on different dates.

TOOLS USED:

- whois
- the harvester<to find email,sub domain...etc>
- grabify <to findoout IP>
- recon-ng
- google dorks
- archive.org

THREE
SCANNING NETWORKS

Scanning

Scanning is a process of identifying network and service-related information by communicating with the target. Scanning helps in identifying IP/Hostnames, Ports, Services running on ports, Live hosts, Vulnerable services running on the target network.

Types of Scanning

Different number of scanning procedures are used with the objective to identify hosts, ports, and services in the target network. One of the most common types scanning methods that are available.

Network Scanning

During the network scanning process, attackers gather a list of IP addresses of computers that are live on the target network. The job of the attacker will be easy if he/she can analyze the network structure and services running on each machine.

List of Network Scanners:

- Angry IP Scanner
- Advanced IP Scanner
- Netdiscover
- Autoscan
- hping3
- Nmap

List of Network Scan Methods:

- Ping Sweep

- Arp Scan

What Are Ports and Port Numbers

Ports are virtual entry points to any digital device; devices can communicate with one to another using port, there are virtually 65535 ports available in every device, those can be identified with port numbers, ranging from 0 to 65535.

0 1023 Well known ports

1024 49135 Random ports

49136 65535 Experimental ports

Port Scanning

Port scanning is a technique where the attacker will send communication probes to targets to see how the target is responding to them, based on the response attacker will determine what ports are open and several other port details, like service running on the port numbers, and OS the target is running.

List of Port scanners:

- Nmap
- SuperScan
- Strobe
- Zenmap

List of Port Scan methods:

- SYN Scan/Stealth Scan/
- TCP Connect Scan
- ACK Scan
- XMAS Scan
- FIN Scan
- NULL Scan
- OS Detection Scan
- Script Scan
- UDP Scan
- Service Detection Scan

Few Well-Known Ports

Application Port Number(s) Application Port Number(s) FTP 20–21 DNS 53

Telnet 23 IRC 194

SMTP 25 POP3 110
DNS 53 SNMP 161
HTTP 80 HTTPS 443
SSH 22 NetBIOS 139
TFTP 69 SQL 156

For details on other port numbers and services refer **RFC-1700**

Live Host identification scan

Identifying the turned-on computers by sending ICMP packets or ARP packets or some other kind of packets is called Live Host Identification Scan.

ICMP

ICMP stands for Internet Control Messaging Protocol; this is widely used for internet communication troubleshooting or to generate errors related to IP operations, this will send packets to the target machine and will see whether the packets are delivered or not.

TCP

Transmission Control Protocol (TCP), which is a widely used protocol for data transmission over a network. This protocol establishes a reliable connection between two hosts before transmitting data, to ensure that data transmitted over the network reaches the destination without fail. TCP also known as a connection-oriented protocol, establishes a reliable connection between sender and receiver. TCP provides error and flow control mechanisms which help in orderly transmission of data and retransmission of lost packets.

UDP

UDP stands for User Datagram Protocol, which is connectionless protocol, mostly used for connections that can tolerate data loss. UDP is used by applications on the internet that offer voice and video communications, which can suffer some data loss without adversely affecting the quality. UDP does not provide error and flow control mechanisms because of which it does not require a connection before transmitting data over the network.

TCP 3-way Handshake

To start a proper TCP conversation, the sender and receiver perform 3- way handshake before exchanging data over the network. It is a process used by two hosts to agree upon some protocol stack to start sharing data. Following image represents the process of 3-way handshake.

TCP COMMUNICATION FLAGS

1. SYN (Synchronize): SYN flags will be used to initiate a data transfer of the start of a communication process.

2. ACK (Acknowledgement): ACK flags will be used to send the receipt of successful packet transmission.

3. FIN (Finish): FIN flags will be used to close or finish an existed packet transmission. No more packets to be received.

4. RST (Reset): RST flags will be used to terminate or reset a connection.

5. URG (Urgent): Data in this flagged packet should be processed immediately.

6. PSH (Push): Sends all buffered data immediately.

Types of Port Scanning Techniques

- **TCP Connect Scan / Full Open Scan** Nmap directly communicates with the operating system to establish a connection with the target machine and port by issuing the connect system call.
- **SYN Scan / Half-Open Scan / Stealth Scan** SYN scan is the most popular scan option. It can scan thousands of ports in a short period on a fast network not hampered by restrictive firewalls.
- **ACK Scan/Firewall Detection** This scan is different from others scanning operations discussed before; it never determines open ports. It is used to identify firewall rules, determining the type of firewall and identify filtered ports.
- **XMAS Scan** The Xmas-Tree scan sends a TCP packet with the following flags:

URG — Indicates that the data is urgent and should be processed immediately
PSH — Forces data to a buffer
FIN — Used when finishing a TCP session

- **FIN Scan** FIN scan, which attempts to close a connection that isn't open. The operating system generates an error if service is not running on target port. If a service is listening, the operating system will silently drop the incoming packet. Therefore, no response indicates a listening service at the port.
- **NULL Scan** A data packet with zero flag values will be sent to a TCP port. (In a regular TCP communication, at least one bit or flag is set). In TCP connect / SYN scans, a response indicates an open port, but in a NULL scan, a response indicates a closed port.

Importance of Scanning

Scanning will provide an exact outline of the network structure of the target workspace. It is beneficial for hacking target servers or individual computers. Scanning will provide a blueprint of entire network and details about devices running on the network, information related to network topology and helps in deciding what operating system is running on target computers.

Countermeasures

- Block ICMP and UDP inbound.
- Disable unused ports with support of policy settings.
- Block internal IP addresses from coming inbound.
- Change system and application banners to counter software detection attacks.
- Always use a genuine operating system, update it frequently.

- Use IDS & IPS to detect and prevent attacks.
- Use "duckduckgo" or "StartPage" search engine to protect privacy.

FOUR

ENUMERATION

Enumeration

Enumeration is the process of establishing an active connection to the target host to discover potential attack vectors in the computer system, information gained at this phase can be used for further exploitation of the system. It is often considered as a critical phase because few pieces of information gathered in this phase can help us directly exploit the target computer.

Information gathered in this phase

1. Usernames, Group names
2. Hostnames
3. Network shares and services
4. IPtables and routing tables
5. Service settings and Audit configurations
6. Application and banners
7. SNMP and DNS Details

NetBIOS enumeration

NetBIOS stands for Network Basic Input Output System. It allows computers to communicate over a LAN to share files and devices like printers. NetBIOS names are used to identify network devices over TCP/IP.

NetBIOS Name List:

Name NetBIOS code NetBIOS code Information Obtained

<hostname> <00> UNIQUE Hostname

<domain> <00> GROUP Domain name

<host name> <03> UNIQUE Messenger service running for that computer <user name> <03> UNIQUE Messenger service running for that individual logged-in user

Benefits of NetBIOS Enumeration:

1. Information related to computers that belong to a domain.
2. Details related to shares on computers in the network.
3. Extracting policies and passwords.

SMB Enumeration:

SMB stands for Server Message Block. It is mainly used for providing shared access to files, printers and miscellaneous communications between nodes on a network. It also provides an authenticated inter-process communication mechanism.

DNS Enumeration :

DNS enumeration retrieves information regarding all the DNS servers and their corresponding records related to an organization. DNS enumeration will yield usernames, computer names, and IP addresses of potential target systems. DNS - Domain Name Servers The Internet equivalent of the phone book. They maintain the directory of domain names & translate them to internet protocol addresses.

DNS Records:

The list of DNS records provides an overview of types of resource records stored in the zone files of the domain name system. The DNS implements a distributed, hierarchical and redundant database for information associated with internet domain names & addresses.

DNS record types and their uses

Record Description

A (Address) It maps hostnames to IPv4 address.

SOA (Start of Authority) It identifies the DNS server responsible for the domain information.

CNAME (Canonical Name) It Provides additional names or aliases for the address.

AAAA (Address) It maps hostnames to IPv6 address.

MX (Mail exchange) It Identifies the mail server for the domain

SRV (Service) It Identifies services such as directory services

PTR (Pointer) It Maps IP address to hostnames

NS (Nameserver) It Identifies other name servers for the domain

DNS Zone Transfer

- Used to replicate DNS data across some DNS Servers or to backup DNS files. A user or server will perform a specific zone transfer request from a name server.
- DNS servers should not permit zone transfers towards any IP address from the Internet.
- Since zone files contain complete information about domain names, subdomains and IP addresses configured on the target name server, finding this information is useful for increasing your attack surface and for better understanding the internal structure of the target company.
- We can identify hidden subdomains, development servers information, and internal IP addresses, etc.

- Information gathered from zone files can be useful for attackers to implement various attacks against the target company, like targeting test or development servers which are less secure.

NTP Enumeration

NTP (Network Time Protocol) utilizes UDP port 123. Through NTP enumeration you can gather information such as a list of hosts connected to NTP server, IP addresses, system names, and operating systems running on the client system in a network. All this information can be enumerated by querying the server.

SNMP Enumeration

Simple Network Management Protocol is an application layer protocol which uses UDP protocol to maintain and manage routers, hubs, switches and other network devices. SNMP is a popular protocol found enabled on a variety of operating systems like Windows Server, Linux & UNIX servers as well as network devices.

SMTP Enumeration

SMTP enumeration allows us to determine valid users on the SMTP server. With the help of built-in SMTP commands, we can gather useful information.

1. VRFY - Is used for validating users.
2. EXPN – Reveals the actual delivery address of mailing lists.
3. RCPT TO - It defines the recipients of the message.

Countermeasures

- Install IDS & IPS to detect and stop Enumerating attacks done on any ports.
- Install honeypot application in a proxy server to give false information to the hacker.
- Upload robots.txt file in the website to stop Footprinting of directories.
- Enable DNSSec option in server OS to avoid information leakage through DNS server.
- Hosts can be locked down and securely configured and patched. Limit services to only those needed.
- Network services can be locked down and made not to give up as much useful information to a hacker.
- Changing default security configuration is very important.
- Block ports to unknown hosts.
- Turn off file and print sharing services in windows.
- Prevent DNS zone transfers to unknown hosts

FIVE
VULNERABILITY ANALYSIS

Vulnerability:

A bug or flaw or a state of being exposed which leads to a critical hacking attack from the Hacker is called Vulnerability.

Vulnerability Research :

It is the process by which security flaws in technology are identified. Vulnerability research does not always involve reverse engineering, code analysis, etc. Performing vulnerability research against technology pre-release enables technology vendors to provide their customers with higher quality products and higher levels of trust and security.

List of vulnerability research websites:

- securityfocus.com
- vulnerability-lab.com
- us-cert.gov
- packetstormsecurity.com
- nvd.nist.gov
- cvedetails.com

Vulnerability Analysis

Vulnerability analysis is the process of defining, identifying, classifying and prioritizing vulnerabilities in computer systems, applications or network infrastructure. This phase allows the organization to perform security assessment with the necessary knowledge, awareness and risk background to understand the threats and react appropriately.

Attackers perform vulnerability analysis to identify security loopholes in the target organization's network or communication infrastructure. Attackers take advantage of identified vulnerabilities to perform further exploitation of that target network.

The vulnerability scanner (software) compares details about the target attack surface to a database of information about known security vulnerabilities in services and ports, anomalies in packet construction, and potential paths to exploitable programs or scripts.

Objectives

- Identify vulnerabilities ranging from critical design flaws to simple misconfigurations.
- Document the vulnerabilities so that the developers and networks administrators can easily identify and reproduce the findings.
- Create guidance to assist network administrators and developers with remediating the identified vulnerabilities

Types of Vulnerability Assessments

- External Scans
- Internal Scans
- Environment Scans
- Host assessment
- Network assessment
- Database assessment

Common types of Vulnerabilities

- Missing data encryption
- SQL injection
- Buffer-overflow
- Missing authentication for critical functions
- Missing authorization
- Unrestricted upload of dangerous file types
- Cross-site request forgery
- Download of codes without integrity checks
- Weak passwords
- Path/Directory traversal

List of network vulnerability scanners

- Nessus
- GFI LanGuard - Scans both Hardware & Software Vulnerabilities.
- Qualys guard - Works both on LAN & WAN
- Saint
- Nexpose - Paid and free solution available from Offensive security
- Core impact - Scanner and Exploit framework
- OpenVAS

Types of Vulnerability Assessment Reports

- Technical Report - Includes detailed description related to vulnerabilities found on the target computer(s)
- Non-Technical Report - Brief report on vulnerabilities found on the target computer(s). This report includes graphs and charts that are easy to understand the risk.

CVE (Common Vulnerabilities and Exposures)

CVE is a dictionary of standardized identifiers for common software vulnerabilities and exposures. CVE IDs, i.e., CVE-2018-1002100 which are assigned by CVE Numbering Authorities from around the world, ensures confidence when used to share information about a unique software or firmware vulnerability, provides a baseline for tool evaluation, and enables data exchange. CVE IDs act as a benchmark for evaluating security services.

CVSS (Common Vulnerability Scoring System)

CVSS is a published standard that provides an open framework for communicating the characteristics and impacts of IT vulnerabilities. Its quantitative model ensures accurate measurement while enabling users to see the underlying vulnerability characteristics that were used to generate the scores. The National Vulnerability Database (NVD) provides CVSS scores for almost all known vulnerabilities. CVSS assessment consists of three metrics for measuring vulnerabilities

1. Base Metrics: It represents the inherent qualities of a vulnerability
2. Temporal Metrics: It represents the features that keep on changing during the lifetime of a vulnerability.
3. Environmental Metrics: It represents the vulnerabilities that are based on a particular environment or implementation.

Each metrics sets a score from 1-10, ten being the most severe. CVSS score is calculated and generated by a vector string, which represents the numerical score for each group in the form of a block of text. CVSS calculator is developed to rank the security vulnerabilities and provide the user with overall severity and risk related to the vulnerability.

SIX
SYSTEM HACKING

System Hacking

System hacking is the process of trying to compromise the target system with the help of the information we collect from the pre-attack phases (Footprinting and scanning).

Metasploit

Metasploit is a Framework used for developing and executing exploit code against a remote target machine.

Metasploit Framework contains following modules

- Exploits
- Payloads
- Auxiliary
- Encoders
- Post
- Nop's

Components of the Metasploit:

- Msfconsole
- Msfvenom
- Armitage

Exploit

Exploits can help gain superuser-level access to a computer system. Hackers manage to gain low-level access; then they try to escalate privileges to the highest level (root). The exploit becomes unusable; once the vulnerability is fixed through a patch

Exploits are Classified based on how the exploit communicate with the vulnerable software.

- A remote exploit works over a network and exploits the security vulnerability without any prior access to the vulnerable system.
- A local exploit requires prior access to the vulnerable system and escalate the privileges of the person running the exploit.

Payload

The payload is the piece of code in the exploit which performs a malicious action, i.e., deleting data, providing the remote connection, sending spam or encrypting data.

Types of Payload :

The Metasploit framework has three different types of payloads

1. Singles
2. Stagers
3. Stages

Single Payload

Singles are self-contained payloads. They perform a simple task like adding a user to the target computer and running executable files in the victim's computer. These kinds of payloads can be caught with non-Metasploit handlers such as netcat. These payloads are more stable because they contain everything in one.

Stager payload

Stager payloads are used to set up a network connection between the attacker and victim and provide the remote connection to execute commands. It is difficult to do both of these well, so the result is multiple similar stagers. Metasploit will use the stagers to create the buffer memory in a small portion of memory; these stagers are responsible for downloading a large payload (the stage), injecting it into memory, and passing execution to it.

Stage payload

Stage Payloads are the components of the stagers that are downloaded in the exploited pc by the Stagers. The various payload stages provide the advanced features with no size limit such as Meterpreter, VNC injection, etc.

Escalating Privileges :

Privilege escalation is a technique to exploit existing vulnerabilities in design, misconfigurations in an operating system or in any installed applications to gain elevated access to resources that are usually protected from an application or user.

Vertical Privilege Escalation

The attacker grants himself higher privileges. Privilege escalation is typically achieved by performing kernel-level operations that allow the attacker to run unauthorized code.

Horizontal Privilege Escalation

Attacker's use the same level of privileges he/she already has been granted, but assume the identity of another user with similar privileges.

Password Cracking

In password cracking, hackers use a different kind of attacks to know the target computer login password so that they can gain complete access.

Types of passwords

Passwords with only letters Ex: admin

Passwords with letters and numbers Ex: admin123

Passwords with letters and special characters Ex: admin@

Passwords with only numbers Ex: 6842

Passwords with only special characters Ex: @!#$%%^

Passwords with numbers and special characters Ex: 1234!@#$

Passwords with letters, numbers and special characters Ex: admin@123

Methods to Crack password

Password Guessing – Not a technique, but usually the first thing that every criminal will try to do.

Brute Force Attack – All possible permutations & combinations of the keyboard are tried as the victim's password. All passwords have to be some permutation or combination of victim's keyboard characters.

Dictionary Based Attack – All words in the dictionary are tried as the victim's password.

Syllable attack – Combination of both, brute force attack and a dictionary attack. This is often used when the password is a nonexistent word.

Default Passwords – Manufacturers configure the hardware or software with default passwords and settings. We can get default passwords online for devices (http://defaultpassword.us/).

Data Sniffing – Data sniffer to record passwords being sent across the LAN network in plaintext format.

Countermeasures

- Keep Operating system software updated (patched).
- Use stronger authentication methods.
- Enable security auditing to help monitor attacks.
- Avoid storing user names/password on disk.
- Change passwords on a frequent basis.
- Build user awareness on social engineering attack

SEVEN
MALWARE THREATS

Malware

Malware (malicious software) is a type of program that combines malicious code with genuine application to perform unauthorized operations in such a way that it can take control of a system or cause damage.

Types of Malware

1. Trojan
2. Virus
3. Worm
4. Rootkits
5. Spyware
6. Ransomware
7. Adware
8. Backdoor

Fileless Malware:

Fileless Malware infects legitimate software's and applications such as Microsoft Word, PDF documents, flash, PowerShell, macros etc., to perform various malicious activities. Attackers commonly use social engineering techniques to spread Fileless malware. Fileless malware also known as nomalware will leave no traces making it difficult for anti-virus programs to detect.

Trojan

Trojan is a malicious program, bound with a harmless application program or data in such a way that it can help an attacker gain control and cause damage to the targeted machine. Malware tries to steal victim's confidential information and sends back to the attacker.

Symptoms of Trojan Attack

- Computer browser is redirected to unknown pages.
- Strange chat boxes appear on computer screen.
- Reversing the functions of the right and left mouse buttons.
- Abnormal activity by the modem, network adapter, or hard drive.
- The account passwords changes.
- The ISP complains to the target that your computer is performing unauthorized network scanning.
- An attacker can gain access to personal information about a target

Trojan Detection

- Scan for suspicious OPEN PORTS
- Scan for suspicious RUNNING PROCESSES
- Scan for suspicious DEVICE DRIVERS INSTALLED
- Scan for suspicious REGISTRY ENTRIES
- Scan for suspicious WINDOWS SERVICES
- Scan for suspicious STARTUP PROGRAMS
- Scan for suspicious NETWORK ACTIVITIES

Checking for Open Ports

- By using the netstat tool to check for open ports, the connection established ports

Checking for suspicious Processes

- By using the process monitor tool, we verify for suspicious processes

Check for Suspicious Driver

- By using the Driver view tool to check for the Suspicious drivers in the system

Virus

VIRUS stands for Vital Information Resource Under Seize. The virus can self-replicate by producing a copy of itself and attaching to another program, computer boot sector or a document.

Creating a Virus using Batch file programming or bash commands

Batch file programming can be used to automate several jobs in windows operating system, which means the repetitive tasks can be written in a file by the administrators to simplify the job just by running the file instead of executing command separately.

Shell scripting performs the similar job in Linux environment to automate the execution of simple commands. Hackers take advantage of batch or shell scripting knowledge to create dangerous viruses which can destroy data on a victim machine or can consume all the PC resources to make the PC either crash or slow down.

Worms

Worms are malicious programs that replicate and spread across the network connections independently without human restrictions to infect computers.

Rootkit

Rootkit is a malicious program that has the ability to hide its presence from the user (victim) and perform malicious activities to grant full access of the infected computer to the attacker.

Spyware

Spyware is a program that records user interaction with the computer, without their knowledge and sends them to the remote attackers over the internet. Spyware hides its process, files, and other objects to avoid detection and removal.

Ransomware

Ransomware is a malware that can restrict access to computer system files and folders and demands an online ransom payment to the malware creator to remove the restrictions.

Adware

Adware is designed to display unwanted advertisements on the browser which redirects users search requests to malicious web pages that forces them to download malware on to their computers. Adware can also be used to collect users search habits.

Backdoor

A backdoor is a piece of code executed on victim computer system by an attacker to bypass standard authentication and maintain secure unauthorized access to remote desktop.

Countermeasures

- Do not download email attachments received from unknown senders.
- Block unnecessary ports running vulnerable services.
- Avoid downloading and executing applications from untrusted sources.
- Restrict permissions within the desktop environment to prevent malicious applications installation.
- Run host-based antivirus, firewall, and intrusion detection software.
- Manage local workstation file integrity through checksums, auditing, and port scanning

EIGHT
SNIFFING

Sniffing

Sniffing is the process of monitoring and capturing all data packets passing through a given network. Sniffing is a form of wiretap applied to computer networks. We can sniff data packets using tools like Wireshark. Any protocol that do not encrypt data are vulnerable to sniffing attacks. Attackers use sniffers to capture data packets containing sensitive information such as passwords, account information, etc.

Sniffers Works in the Datalink Layer. If the initial layer is compromised, then the rest of the layers are also compromised in the OSI model

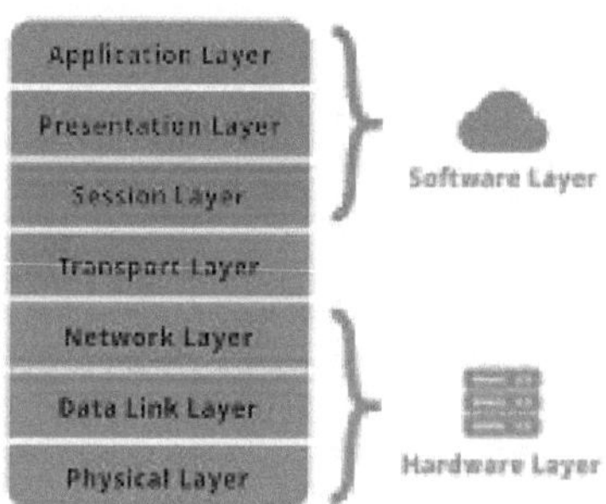

Sniffer

A sniffer is a software tool that monitors the data flowing through computer network links in real time. It can be a self-contained software program or a hardware device with the appropriate software or firmware to perform sniffing.

Sniffers can capture copies of data packets without redirecting or altering it. Some sniffers work only with TCP/IP packets, but the more sophisticated tools can work with many other network protocols and at lower levels, including ethernet frames.

Types of sniffing

Sniffing is classified into two types based on the way they interact with the data packet to capture and provide the user the ability to alter the packet.

- Active sniffing
- Passive sniffing

Active Sniffing

Active Sniffing involves injecting address resolution (ARP) packets into the network to modify Content Addressable Memory (CAM) Table which resides in the switch; CAM keeps track of which host is connected to which port on the switched network.

Passive sniffing

Passive sniffing involves listening and capturing traffic, in a network connected by hubs.

Protocols Vulnerable to Sniffing

HTTP - 80
FTP - 20/21
POP3 - 110
SMTP - 25
RDP - 3389
SSH - 22
NTP - 123
Telnet - 23
IMAP - 123
SNMP - 25

Port Mirroring (SPAN port)

Port mirroring is used by the network switch to send a copy of all network traffic to SPAN port on the switch. This is commonly used for monitoring network traffic by system administrators to detect suspicious activities in the network.

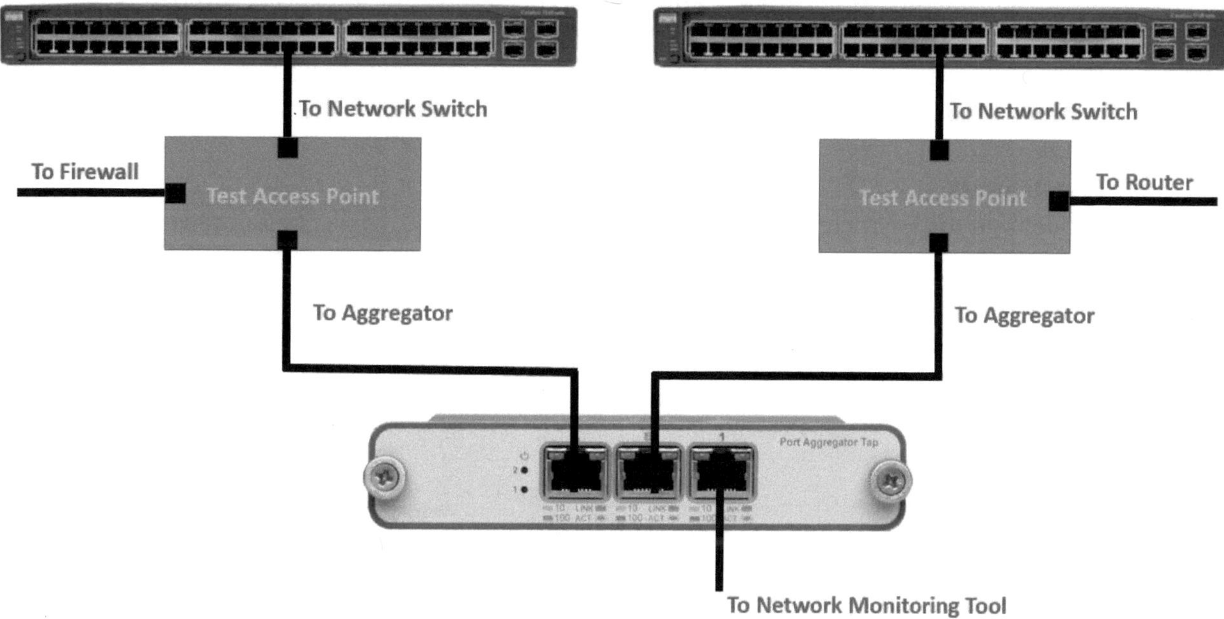

Address Resolution Protocol

Address Resolution Protocol (ARP) is a communication protocol used for discovering the link layer address, such as a MAC address, associated with a given network layer address. This mapping is a critical function in the Internet Protocol suite. It is communicated within the boundaries of a single network never routed across internetworking nodes. ARP uses a simple message format containing one address resolution request or response. The size of the ARP message depends on the link layer and network layer address sizes.

ARP spoofing

In computer networking, ARP spoofing is a technique by which an attacker sends spoofed ARP messages onto a local area network. Generally, the aim is to associate the attacker's MAC address with the IP address of another host, such as the default gateway, causing any traffic meant for that IP address to be sent to the attacker instead.

ARP spoofing may allow an attacker to intercept data frames on a network, modify the traffic, or stop all traffic. Often this attack leads to other attacks, such as Denial of service (DoS), Man in the middle (MITM), or Session hijacking attacks.

DNS spoofing

DNS spoofing is a technique of introducing corrupt Domain Name System details into the DNS resolver cache causing the name server to return an incorrect result record. This results in traffic being diverted to the attacker's computer.

A domain name system translates human-readable domain name into a numerical IP address that is used to route communications between nodes. If a DNS server is poisoned, it returns an incorrect IP address that diverts the traffic to another computer.

Man in the Middle attack

Man in the Middle attack is where an attacker positions himself in a conversation between a user and an application either to eavesdrop or to impersonate regular conversations. The attacker tries to steal personal information, such as login credentials, account details, and credit card numbers. Information obtained during attacks can be used to perform identity theft, unapproved fund transfers or an illicit password change.

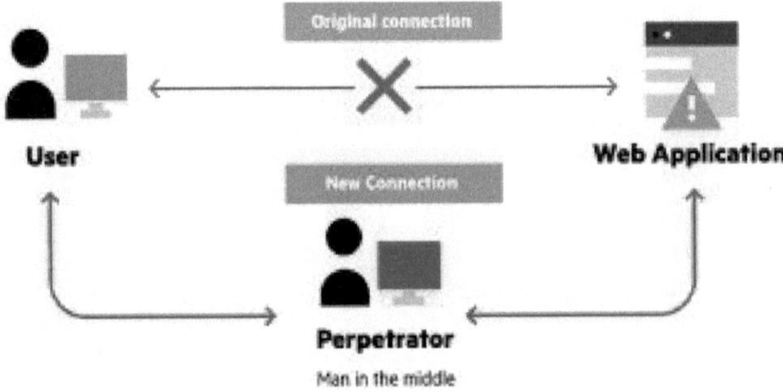

Sniffing Detection Methods

1. Observing Network Traffic
2. Observing ARP Table to Detect ARP Poisoning
3. XARP Advanced ARP Poisoning Detection Tool

Countermeasures

- Use HTTPS instead of HTTP to protect usernames and passwords.
- Use switch instead of the hub as switch delivers data only to the intended recipient.
- Use SFTP, instead of FTP for secure transfer of files.
- Use PGP and S/MIME, VPN, IPsec, SSL/TLS, SSH and One-time passwords.
- Always encrypt the wireless traffic with a strong encryption protocol such as WPA and WPA2.
- Retrieve MAC directly from NIC instead of OS; this prevents MAC address spoofing.

- Use tools to determine if any NIC's are running in the promiscuous mode.

NINE
SOCIAL ENGINEERING

Social engineering

Social engineering is an art of exploiting humans to gain sensitive information. This technique involves tricking people into breaking standard security procedures. It is a most significant threat in any organization. Common targets of social engineering include help desk personnel, technical support executives, system administrators, etc.

NOTE: YouTube Reference: The Real Hustle

Types of Social engineering

Social engineering is classified based on the techniques used to attack or commit fraud on the victim to steal the sensitive information. Types of social engineering attacks are:

- Human-based
- Computer-based
- Mobile-based

Human-Based

In human-based social engineering attacks, the social engineer interacts directly with the target to get sensitive information by performing the various techniques such as

- Shoulder surfing
- Dumpster diving
- Tailgating
- Piggybacking

Computer Based

Computer-based social engineering attacks are carried out with the help of computer software to gain access to the desired information. Some of these attack types are listed as follows:

- Phishing
- Spam mail
- Popup windows

Mobile Based

In mobile-based social engineering attacks, attackers take advantage of malicious mobile applications to gain access to the desired information. Some of the attack types are listed as follows:

- SMishing
- Publish malicious apps
- Repacking legitimate apps

Exploiting Human Using Social engineering

Social engineering and the human element are common ways to gain access to a network, database, or building. Major cyber incidents happen as the result of an attacker gaining initial access using social engineering technique, usually by convincing an insider to unwittingly download or install a piece of malware that opens up the target network to the attacker.

Attackers employ many tricks to try to get a human target to provide them with information or access. They appeal to ego, financial need, curiosity, humanity, or job duties all with the goal of getting the target to either click on a link that redirects the target to a malicious website or opens an attachment that contains malware.

Humans continue to be the weak link. No matter how secure a network, device, system, or organization is from a technical point of view, humans can often be exploited.

- Individuals should be vigilant regarding emails
- unsolicited phone calls that attempt to get people to reveal sensitive information.
- Companies should regularly provide security awareness training to employees.
- Lack of the security policies
- Unregulated access to information

Eavesdropping

Eavesdropping is a technique used by attackers to intercept unauthorized and private communication, such as a phone call, instant message, video conference or fax transmission. This is done by directly listening to digital or analog voice communication or by intercepting or sniffing data relating to any form of communication.

Video Reference: https://www.youtube.com/watch?v=1ASIxT-VGUY

Enter Caption

Dumpster diving

Dumpster diving is looking for treasure in someone else's trash. (A dumpster is a large trash container). In Information Technology, dumpster diving refers to a technique used to retrieve information that could be used to perform attacks on a computer network. Dumpster diving is not limited to searching through the trash for information like access codes or passwords written down on sticky notes Reference:https://www.social-engineer.org/framework/informationgathering/dumpster-diving/

Shoulder Surfing

Shoulder surfing is noting but direct observation, such as looking over someone's shoulder, to grab sensitive details. It is commonly used while someone enters passwords, PIN numbers, security codes at ATMs or on their personal computers.

Reference: https://www.socialengineer.org/framework/information-gathering/physicalmethods-of-information-gathering/

Tailgating and Piggybacking

A person tags himself with another person who is authorized to gain access into a restricted area, or pass a specific checkpoint is known as Tailgating/Piggybacking. Tailgating implies without consent while piggybacking means approval of the authorized person.

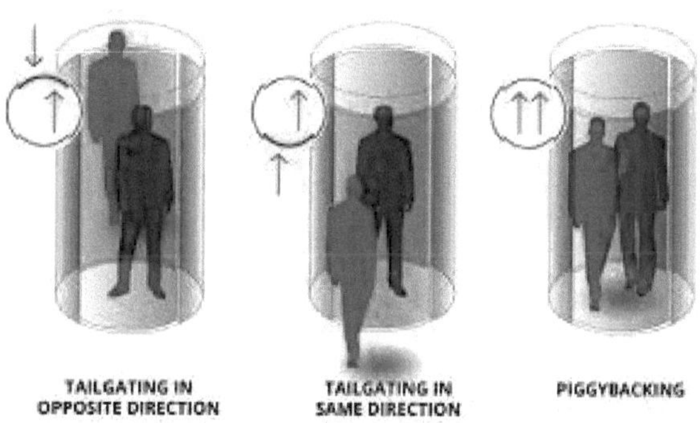

Phishing

Phishing is the attempt to acquire sensitive information such as usernames, passwords, and credit card details (and sometimes, financial information), often for malicious reasons, by masquerading as a trustworthy entity in electronic communication.

Reference: https://www.social-engineer.org/framework/attack-vectors/phishing-attacks2/

Spear phishing

Spear phishing is a variation on phishing in which hackers send emails to groups of people with specific common characteristics or other identifiers. Spear phishing emails appear to come from a trusted source but are designed to help hackers obtain trade secrets or other classified information.

Countermeasures

1. Employees in an organization should be aware of security policies and procedures.
2. Secure or shred all the documents containing private information.
3. Protect your personal information from being published.
4. Never store personal/banking information on the mobile device.

TEN
DENIAL OF SERVICE

Denial of Service

a Denial of service (DoS) attack is an attempt to make a machine or network resource unavailable to its intended users, such as to temporarily or indefinitely interrupt or suspend services of a host connected to the Internet.

Distributed Denial Of service

A distributed denial-of-service (DDoS) attack occurs when multiple systems flood the targeted system with traffic to make the resources unavailable to its intended users, usually one or more web servers. Such an attack is often the result of multiple compromised systems (for example a botnet) flooding the.

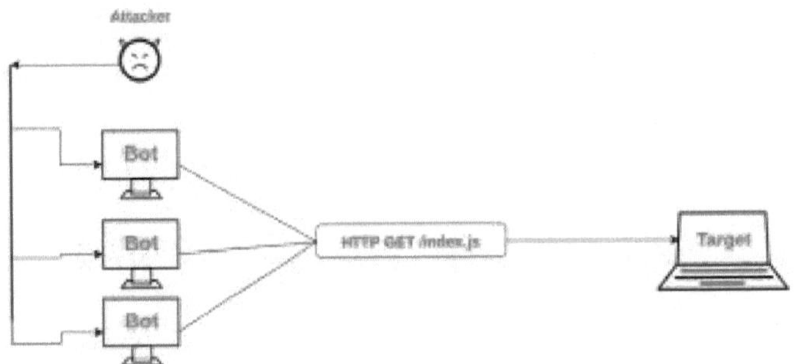

Botnet

A botnet is a collection of Internet-connected devices that are infected and controlled by a common type of malware each of which is running one or more bots. Infected machines are controlled remotely. Botnet infections are usually spread through malware, such as a trojan horse. Botnet malware is typically designed to automatically scan systems and devices for common vulnerabilities that haven't been patched. Botnet malware may also scan for ineffective or outdated security products, such as firewalls or antivirus software. Common tasks executed by botnets include:

- Using the machine's power to assist in distributed denial-of-service (DDoS).
- Generating spam emails.
- Internet traffic generation on a third-party website.
- Replacing banner ads in a web browser.

Exploiting System and Application Level Vulnerabilities

In this method, either the operating system or the application software will have bugs which will cause a denial of service situation. Once an attacker finds this vulnerability, he has to find out the working exploit code for the vulnerability, if an attacker finds the exploit code, he can use it to DOS the target without any further problems.

TCP SYN Flood

TCP SYN flood is a type of Distributed Denial of Service (DDoS) attack that exploits part of the normal TCP three-way handshake to consume resources on the targeted server and render it unresponsive. With SYN flood DDoS, the attacker sends TCP connection requests faster than the targeted machine can process them, causing network saturation.

In a SYN flood attack, the attacker sends repeated SYN packets to every port on the targeted server, using a fake IP address. The server receives multiple, apparently legitimate requests to establish communication. It responds to each attempt with a SYN-ACK packet from each open port.

The attacker either does not send the expected ACK or if the IP address is spoofed never receives the SYN-ACK in the first place. Either way, the server under attack will wait for an acknowledgment for its SYN-ACK packet for some time. During this time, the server cannot close down the connection by sending RST packet, and the connection stays open. Before the connection can time out, another SYN packet will arrive. This leaves an increasingly large number of connections half-open

UDP Flood

UDP flood is a type of Denial of Service (DoS) attack in which the attacker sends a request to random ports on the targeted host with IP packets containing UDP datagrams.

The receiving host checks for applications associated with these datagrams and if no application is associated with the request, then it sends back a "Destination Unreachable" packet. As more and more UDP packets are received which need to be answered, the system becomes overwhelmed and unresponsive to other clients. The attacker may also spoof the IP address of the packets, both to make sure that the return ICMP packets do not reach their host, to anonymize the attack.

User Datagram Protocol (UDP) is a connectionless and session less networking protocol. Since UDP traffic does not require a three-way handshake like TCP, it runs with lower overhead and is ideal for traffic that does not need to be checked and rechecked, such as chat or VoIP.

In the absence of an initial handshake, to establish a valid connection, a high volume of traffic can be sent over UDP channels to any host, with no built-in protection to limit the rate of the UDP DoS flood. This means that UDP flood attacks are highly-effective.

Some UDP flood attacks can take the form of DNS amplification attacks. Where UDP does not define specific packet formats, and thus attackers can create large packets fill them with junk text or numbers and send them out to the host under attack

. When the attacked host receives the garbage-filled UDP packets to a given port, it checks for the application listening at that port, which is associated with the packet's contents. When it observes that, no associated application is listening, it replies with an ICMP Destination Unreachable packet.

HTTP Flood

HTTP flood is a type of Distributed Denial of Service (DDoS) attack in which the attacker sends seemingly legitimate HTTP GET or POST requests to a target web server or application. HTTP client like a web browser communicates with application or server; it sends an HTTP request. A GET request is used to retrieve content while POST requests are used to send dynamically generated content.

The attack is effective when it forces the server or application to allocate the maximum resources possible in response to every single request. For this reason, HTTP flood attacks using POST requests tend to be the most resource effective. POST requests may include parameters that trigger complex server-side processing. On the other hand, HTTP GET based attacks are simple to perform.

Ping of Death

In this method of DOS, the attacker will try to send the large-sized ping packets which the target cannot handle which will cause DOS situation on the target device.

MAC Flooding The Network switch maintains a table called CAM (content addressable memory) to prevent MITM attacks, but it contains a limited number of entries, so when an attacker tries to overload this CAM table with more number of mac addresses than it can handle, sometimes the switch may not be responding to the legitimate requests.

Other types of Flooding

An attacker can use any other protocol vulnerabilities to flood packets to the target device so that the target device will be busy with handling Flood packets and may not respond to the original request made by the legitimate user.

Countermeasures

- DoS detection techniques are based on identifying and discriminating the illegitimate traffic from legitimate packet traffic
- Set up Systems with limited security (Honeypots), to attract an attacker
- FortGuard Anti-DDoS Firewall provides a fundamentally superior approach to mitigating DDoS attacks, with a design that focuses on passing legitimate traffic rather than discarding attack traffic.

ELEVEN
SESSION HI-JACKING

Session

A session stores information (in variables) to be used across multiple pages when a user logs into this online account. Unlike cookies, this information is not stored on the user's computer. Typically maintained by the server, and created on the first request or after an authentication process. The session-id is exchanged between a web browser and the server on every request.

Different ways to exchange session-Id

1. Hidden Form fields
2. Cookies (most common)

Session Token

Session ID or session token is a piece of data that is used in network communications to identify a session. It is used to determine a user that has logged into a website, these IDS or token can be used by an attacker to hijack the session and obtain potential privileges. A session ID is usually a randomly generated string to decrease the probability of obtaining a valid one by means of a brute-force search.

Cookie

Cookies are strings of data that a web server sends to the browser. When a browser requests an object from the same domain in the future, the browser will send the same string of date back to the origin server. The data sent from the web server in the form of an HTTP header called "Set-Cookie". The browser sends the cookie back to the server in an HTTP header called "Cookie". The primary purpose of a cookie is to create customized web pages based on user identities.

Attack Methods

Server-side attacks

- Guessing Session Id - shorter length, predictable

- Session Fixing - predictable, session created before authentication
- Session Sniffing (typical on non-SSL sessions) - same subnet as client or server.

Client-side attacks

- Cross Site Scripting (XSS) - User trusting source, application vulnerability.

Session Sniffing

Attackers can sniff all the traffic from the established TCP session and perform identity theft, information theft, fraud, etc. The attacker steals a valid session ID and uses it to authenticate himself with the server.

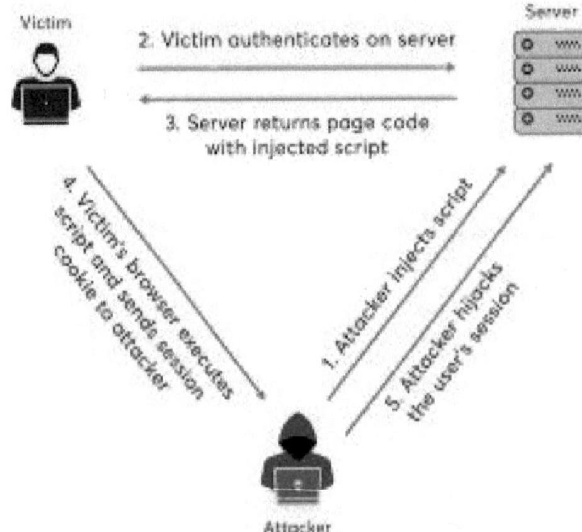

Session Hijacking

Session Hijacking refers stealing of this session-Id and using it to impersonate and access data over a valid TCP communication session between two computers. Application level hijacking is about gaining control over the HTTP user session by obtaining the session IDs.

Countermeasures from a general user point of view

- Do not click on the links that are received through emails.
- Logout from the application instead of closing the browser.
- Always use an updated browser.
- Clear the browsing data like cache, cookies, etc.

Countermeasures from web developer point of view

- Create Session keys with lengthy strings or random number so that it is difficult for an attacker to guess a valid session key.
- Regenerate the session ID after a successful login to prevent session fixation attack (attack starts before user logs in).
- Encrypt the data and session key that is transferred between the user and the web servers.
- Expire the session as soon as the user logs out.
- Use firewalls to prevent the malicious content entering into the network.

TWELVE

EVADING IDS,FIREWALL,HONEYPOTS

Firewall

A firewall is a hardware or software appliance to secure the internal trusted network form the intruders by monitoring and controlling incoming and outgoing network traffic based on predetermined security rules. A firewall typically establishes a barrier between a trusted internal network and an untrusted external network.

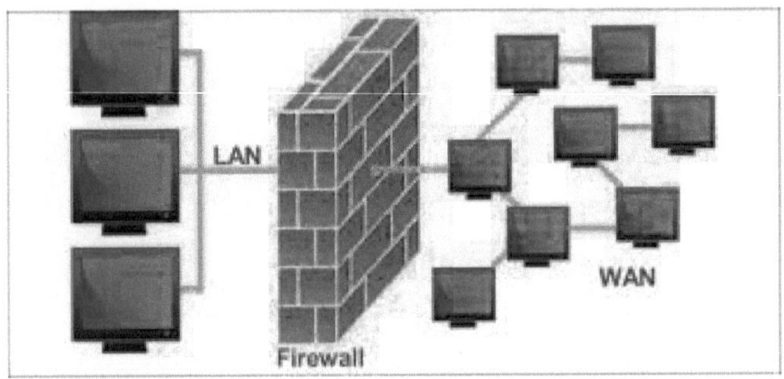

Types of Firewalls

1. Packet filter firewalls
2. Circuit-level gateways
3. Stateful inspection firewalls
4. Application-level gateways

Packet Filter Firewalls

Packet filtering firewall is used to control network access by monitoring outgoing and incoming packets and allowing them to pass or halt based on the source and destination Internet Protocol (IP) addresses, protocols and ports and this work on IP layer of TCP/IP. The packet filtering firewall examines the header of each packet based on a specific set of rules.

Circuit-level gateways

Circuit level gateways work at the session layer of the OSI model; they monitor TCP handshake to determine whether a requested session is legitimate or not. Information passed to a remote computer through a circuit level gateway firewall appears to be originated at user's computer. Firewall technology supervises TCP handshaking among packets to confirm that the session is genuine.

Circuit level gateways are relatively inexpensive and have the advantage of hiding information about the private network. On the other hand, they do not filter individual packets.

Application-level gateways

Application-level gateways can filter packets at the application layer of the OSI model. Application-level gateways examine traffic and filter on application specific commands such as HTTP, POST and GET. This works on the application layer of the TCP/IP Model.

Stateful inspection firewalls

Stateful inspection firewalls combine the aspects of the other three types of firewalls. They filter packets at the network layer, to determine whether session packets are legitimate, and they evaluate the contents of packets at the application layer. Traffic is filtered at three layers based on a wide range of the specified application, session, and packet filtering rules

Types of Firewall Architectures

The different types of firewall architectures are

1. Bastion Host
2. Screened Subnet (DMZ - Demilitarized Zone)
3. Dual-Homed Firewall

Bastion Host

A Bastion host is a computer that is fully exposed to attack. The system is on the public side of the demilitarized zone, unprotected by a firewall or filtering router. Frequently the roles of these systems are critical to the network security system.

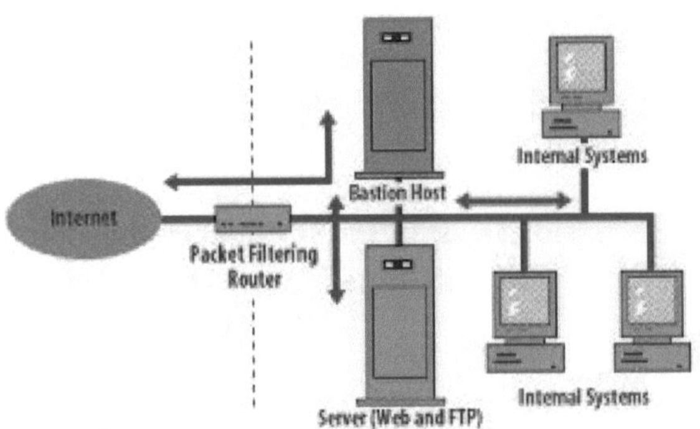

Screened Subnet (DMZ)

A screened subnet (also known as a "triple-homed firewall") is a network architecture that uses a single firewall with three network interfaces. In computer security, a DMZ or demilitarized zone is a physical or logical subnetwork that contains and exposes an organization's external-facing services to a larger and untrusted network, usually the Internet.

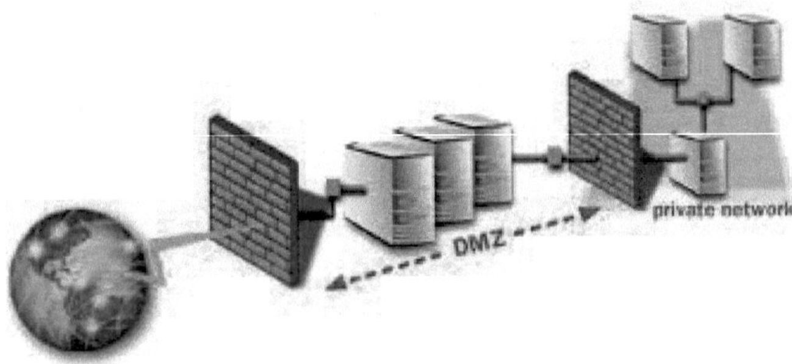

Dual-Homed Firewall A dual-homed host (or dual-homed gateway) is a system fitted with two network interfaces (NICs) that sits between an untrusted network (like the Internet) and trusted network (such as a corporate network) to provide secure access. Dualhomed is a general term for proxies, gateways, firewalls, or any server running security applications or providing security services directly to an untrusted network.

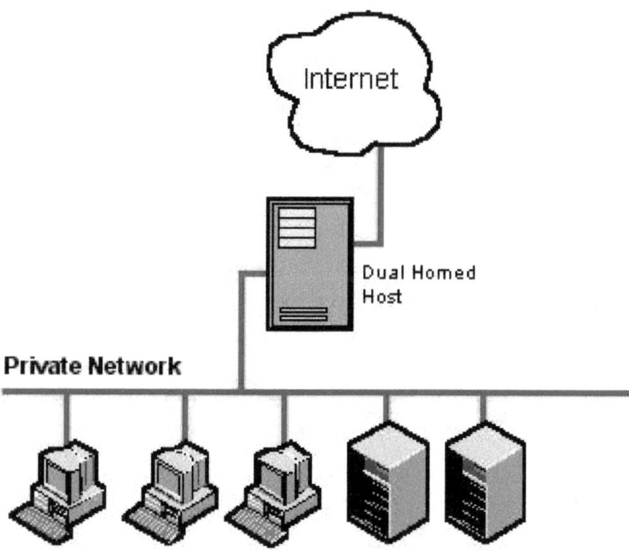

Dual-homed hosts can be seen as a special case of bastion hosts and multihomed hosts. They fall into the category of application-based firewalls. Dualhomed hosts can act as firewalls provided that they do not forward IP datagrams unconditionally.

List of Firewall Products

Software firewalls

- Lavasoft Personal Firewall
- NetLimiter
- Windows Firewall
- ZoneAlarm
- Nftables
- Netfilter/iptables
- IPFilter
- Norton 360
- PeerBlock
- Shorewall

Hardware firewalls

- Clavister
- FortiGate
- Sophos
- Juniper SSG
- Sonicwall
- Barracuda Firewall
- WinGate
- Endian Firewall
- Cisco ASA Firepower
- CiscoPI

Differences between stateful and stateless firewalls

Stateful firewalls monitor all aspects of the traffic streams, their characteristics and communication channels. These firewalls can integrate encryption or tunnels, identify TCP connection stages, packet state and other key status updates.

Stateless firewalls use clues from the destination address, source and other key values to assess whether threats are present, then block those deemed untrusted. Preset rules enforce whether traffic is permitted or denied, but the system is typically unable to determine the difference between truly desired communications and sophisticated attempts to disguise unauthorized communications as trusted ones.

Honeypot

In computer terminology, a honeypot is a computer security mechanism set to detect or deflect attempts at unauthorized access to the information systems. In other words, it is a simple trap to catch the hackers. In honeypots, we will emulate the required devices in an environment, and we will let attackers come there and try to perform attacks. But meanwhile, we will get the identity of the attacker. So that we can take action against attacks. Honeypots are of two types

Low Interaction Honeypot

Low interaction honeypots allow only limited interaction for an attacker. All services offered by a low interaction honeypot are emulated. Thus, these are not themselves vulnerable and will not become infected by the exploit attempted against the vulnerability.

High interaction honeypot

High interaction honeypots make use of the actual vulnerable service or software. These are usually complex as they involve real vulnerable operating systems and applications. In this type of Honeypots, nothing is emulated everything is real and provide a far more detailed picture of how an attack or intrusion progresses or how a particular malware executes in real-time.

List of honeypots

Database Honeypots

- Elastic honey - A simple elastic search honeypot
- NoSQL Honeypot Framework - A framework for NoSQL databases
- ESPot - elasticsearch honeypot

Anti-honeypot stuff

- Kippo detect - This is not a honeypot, but it detects kippo.

ICS/SCADA honeypots

- Conpot - ICS/SCADA honeypot
- Scada-honeynet - Mimics many of the services from a popular PLC and better helps SCADA researchers understand the potential risks of exposed control system devices

Service Honeypots

- Honey NTP - NTP logger/honeypot
- Honeypot camera - Observation camera honeypot
- Troje - A honeypot built around lxc containers. It will run each connection with the service within a separate lxc container.
- Slipm honeypot - A simple low-interaction port monitoring honeypot

Web honeypots

- Glastopf - Web Application Honeypot
- PhpMyAdmin honeypot - A simple and effective phpMyAdmin honeypot
- Servlet pot - Web Application Honeypot
- Node pot - A Nodejs web app NoSQL honeypot framework application
- Basic Auth Pot - HTTP basic authentication honeypot
- Shadow Daemon - A modular Web Application Firewall / High-Interaction Honeypot for PHP, Perl & Python apps

- Google Hack Honeypot - designed to provide reconnaissance against attackers that use search engines as a hacking tool against your resources.
- Smart Honeypot - PHP script demonstrating a smart honeypot
- WP Smart Honeypot - WordPress plugin to reduce comment spam with a smarter honeypot
- Word pot - A WordPress Honeypot
- Bukkit Honeypot - A honeypot plugin for Bukkit
- Laravel Application Honeypot - Simple spam prevention package for Laravel applications
- Stack Honeypot - Inserts a trap for spambots into responses
- Eos Honeypot Bundle - Honeypot type for Symfony2 forms
- Shock pot - WebApp Honeypot for detecting Shell Shock exploit attempts

Intrusion Detection System (IDS)

An intrusion detection system (IDS) is a device or software application that monitors network or computer system operations for malicious activities, policy violations and reports to a controlling station.

Capabilities of IDS

- Monitoring the operation of routers, firewalls, key management servers and files that are needed by other security controls aimed at detecting, preventing or recovering from cyber attacks.
- Including an extensive attack signature database against which information from the system can be matched.
- Recognizing and reporting when the IDS detects that data files have been altered.
- Generating an alarm and notifying the security operations team when there is a security breach.

IDS detection methods Signature-based

Signature-based IDS performs detection of attacks by looking for specific patterns, such as byte sequences in network traffic, or known malicious instruction sequences used by malware. Signature-based IDS is very helpful for detecting already known attacks, but it fails in detecting new attacks, for which no pattern is available. Signatures fall into two categories

Attack signatures - They describe action patterns that may pose a security threat. Typically, they are presented as a time-dependent relationship between a series of activities.

Selected text strings - Signatures to match text strings which look for suspicious action (for example - calling /etc./passwd)

Anomaly-based

Anomaly detectors construct profiles that represent normal usage and then use current behavior data to detect a possible mismatch between profiles and recognize possible attack attempts. In order to match event profiles, the system is required to produce initial user profiles to train the system about legitimate user behaviors, which is a difficult and time-consuming task. Everything that does not match the stored profile is considered to be a suspicious action.

Types of IDS

1. Network-based Intrusion Detection System
2. Host-based Intrusion Detection System

Network-based IDS

NIDS is an IDS which can be configured on a network to monitor intrusions. This will notify the administrators about any possible signature match of attacks.

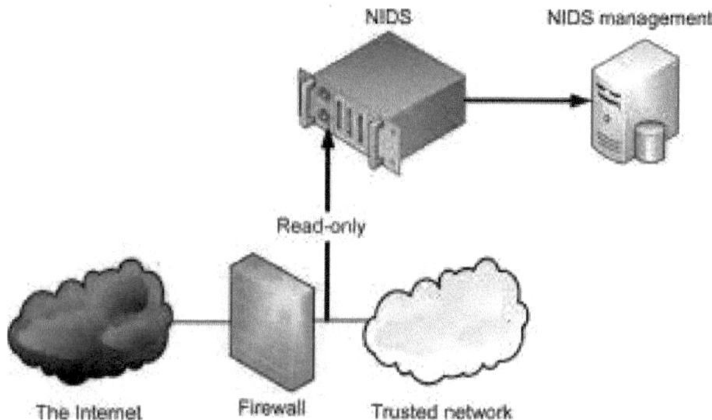

Host-based IDS

HIDS are the IDS systems which will be configured on the standalone machines and will only detect intrusions for that particular machine. HIDS might detect which program accesses what resources and discover malicious attempts, for example, a word-processor has suddenly started modifying the system password database, which can be considered as a malicious attempt on sensitive data stored on the host machine.

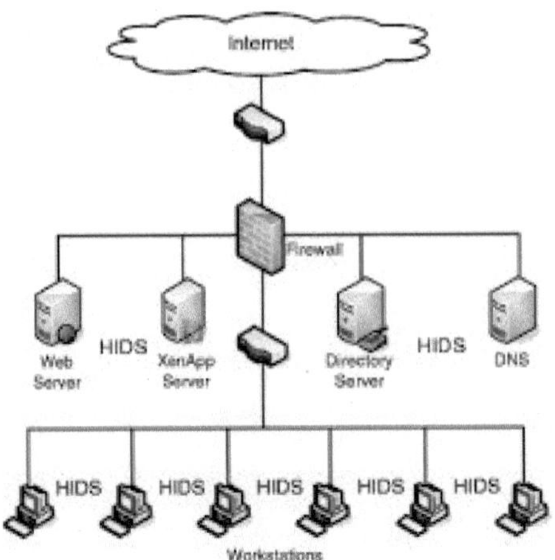

List of Intrusion detection systems

- Snort IDS
- SonicWall
- Juniper
- McAfee Security Agent
- Palo Alto
- Cisco ASA Security Agent

Intrusion Prevention System (IPS)

An Intrusion Prevention System (IPS) is a network security/threat prevention technology that examines network traffic flows to detect and prevent vulnerability exploits. Vulnerability exploits usually come in the form of malicious inputs to a target application or service that attackers use to interrupt and gain control of an application or machine.

The IPS often sits directly behind the firewall and provides a complementary layer of analysis for dangerous content detection. The Intrusion Detection System (IDS) which is a passive system that scans traffic and reports back on threats but the Intrusion Prevention System (IPS) is placed in the direct communication path www.hackerschool.in between source and destination, that can actively analyze and take automated actions on all traffic that enter the network. These actions include:

- Sending an alarm to the administrator

- Dropping the malicious packets
- Blocking traffic from the source address
- Resetting the connection

Types of IPS

Host-based intrusion prevention systems

Host-based intrusion prevention systems are used to protect both servers and workstations through software that runs between your system's applications and OS kernel. The software is preconfigured to determine the protection rules based on intrusion and attack signatures. The HIPS will catch suspicious activity on the system and then, depend on the predefined rules; it will either block or allow the event to happen. HIPS monitor activities such as application or data requests, network connection attempts, and read or write attempts.

Network-based intrusion prevention systems

Network-based intrusion prevention system is a solution for network-based security. NIPS will intercept all network traffic and monitor it for suspicious activity and events, either blocking the requests or passing it. One interesting aspect of NIPS is that if the system finds an offending packet of information it can rewrite the packet so that attempt for the attack will fail, but the organization can mark this event to gather evidence against the intruder, without their knowledge.

IDS vs IPS

Intrusion Detection Systems (IDS) and Intrusion Prevention Systems (IPS) are both parts of the network infrastructure. IDS/IPS compare network packets to a cyberthreat database containing known signatures of cyberattacks — and flag any matching packets.

Both IDS/IPS read network packets and compare the contents to a database of known threats. The primary difference between them is what happens next. IDS are detection and monitoring tools that don't take action on their own. IPS is a control system that accepts or rejects a packet based on the ruleset. IDS require a human or another system to look at the results and determine what actions to take next, which could be a full-time job depending on the amount of network traffic generated each day. IDS make a better post-mortem forensics tool for the CSIRT to use as part of their security incident investigations. The purpose of the IPS, on the other hand, is to catch dangerous packets and drop them before they reach their target. It's more passive than an IDS, simply requiring that the database gets regularly updated with new threat data.

Many IDS/IPS vendors have integrated newer IPS systems with firewalls to create a Unified Threat Management (UTM) technology that combines the functionality of those two similar systems into a single unit. Some systems provide both IDS and IPS functionality in one unit.

Countermeasures

- Shut down switch ports associated with the known attack hosts.

- Perform an in-depth analysis of network traffic to detect all possible threats.
- Use a traffic normalizer to remove potential ambiguity from the packet stream before it reaches to the IDS.
- Harden the security of all communication devices such as modems, routers, switches, etc.

THIRTEEN
HACKING WEB SERVER

Web Servers

Web Server is a computing system that runs on server OS to process the HTTP/HTTPS requests and serve the web pages on the world wide web. The pages delivered are HTML documents, which may include images and scripts in addition to the text content. Clients use a web browser to interact with the web server.

Any computer can be turned into a Web server by installing server software and connecting the machine to the Internet. There are many Web server software applications like Xampp, Apache, Nginx, IIS web server, etc.

How do Web Servers work?

When a user requests a web page hosted on the internet, the web server responds with that requested page. The below image represents this process.

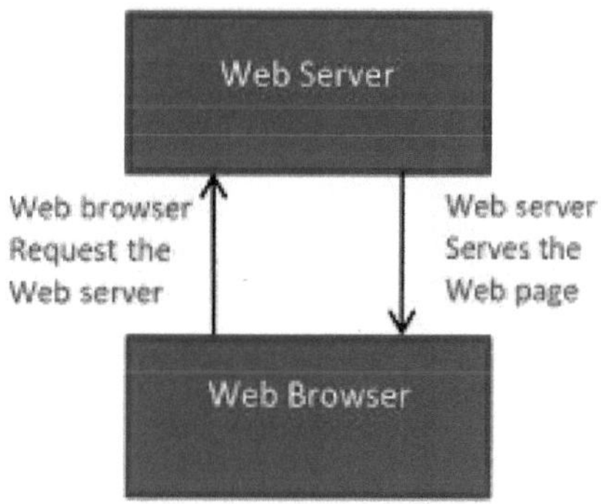

Obtaining the IP Address from domain name:

Web browser first obtains the domain name and resolves it to IP address. It can obtain the IP address in 2 ways:

1. By searching cache.
2. By requesting one or more DNS Servers.

After knowing the IP Address, the browser now demands a full URL from the web server. The web server responds, by sending the requested page to the browser, and if, the web page does not exist, then it will display an appropriate error message. The browser renders the response received from the server to display it on the screen.

List of popular web servers

The following are a list of the common web servers:

Apache – The commonly used web server on the internet. It is cross-platform application software, but it is usually installed on Linux. Most PHP websites are hosted on Apache servers.

Internet Information Services (IIS) – It runs on windows and is the second most used web server on the internet. Most websites built using ASP.Net are hosted on IIS servers.

Apache Tomcat – Java server pages (JSP) websites are hosted on this type of web server.

Other web servers – Novell's Web Server, IBM Lotus Domino servers, Cloudflare web server, Oracle web server, Lightspeed servers, Amazon web server, Google web server, Nginx, etc.

Footprinting Web Server

- Attackers use ID Serve, Netcraft, HTTP Recon, Whois tools to get details about the target server.
- Use robot's exclusion protocol, a standard used by websites to communicate with web crawlers and other web robots to gather some sensitive information.
- This file (robots.txt) will inform the web robot about which areas of the website should not be processed or scanned.
- By performing the DNS enumeration, we can get the dns records and types of servers.

Web Server Vulnerabilities

The following vulnerabilities are most commonly exploited in web servers:

- Improper file and directory permissions.
- Unnecessary services enabled, including content management and remote administration.
- Improper authentication with external systems.
- Default accounts with default or no passwords.
- Misconfiguration in web-server, operating system or network.
- Bugs in server software, OS or web application.

- Lack of security policy and procedures

Types of Attacks possible against Web Servers

Denial of Service Attacks – With this type of attack, the web server may crash or become unavailable to the legitimate users.

Domain Name System Hijacking – In this type of attack, the DNS settings are changed to point victims to the attacker's web server. All the traffic was supposed to hit a malicious server.

Sniffing – Unencrypted data sent over the network may be intercepted and used to gain unauthorized access to the web server.

Defacement – In this type of attack, the attacker takes advantage of vulnerabilities in the web server to replaces the organization's website with a different page that contains the hacker's name, images and may include background music and messages.

Impact of Web Server Attacks

- Easy to compromise user accounts.
- Gaining root access to other applications on servers.
- Access to confidential data (Data tampering/Data theft).
- Perform Web Application attacks.
- The compromised web server can be used to spread malicious software on the internet, which can infect users who visit the compromised website.
- Compromised user data can be used for fraudulent activities.
- An organization's reputation can be ruined.

Identify Vulnerabilities on Web Server

- Perform vulnerability scan to identify weaknesses in a network and determine if the system can be exploited.
- Use vulnerability scanners like Sparta, Nikto, HP Web Inspect, Acunetix Web Vulnerability Scanner to find out hosts, services, and vulnerabilities.
- Sniff the network traffic to identify vulnerabilities on active systems or network services.
- Test the web server infrastructure for any misconfigurations, outdated content, and vulnerabilities.

Webserver response codes

Webserver response codes are also known as Hypertext Transfer Protocol (HTTP) response status codes. Status codes are issued by a server in response to a client's request made to the server. The Internet Assigned Numbers Authority (IANA) maintains the official registry of HTTP status codes.

All HTTP response status codes are separated into five categories. The first digit of the status code specifies one of five standard classes of responses, while the last two digits do not have any classifying or categorization role. There are five classes defined by the standard

- Informational responses (100–199),
- Successful responses (200–299),
- Redirects (300–399),
- Client errors (400–499),
- and Server errors (500–599).

Countermeasures

- Scan for existing vulnerabilities, patch and update the server software regularly.
- Block all unnecessary ports, ICMP traffic, and unnecessary protocols.
- Consistently apply the latest software patches and update system software.
- If remote access is needed, make sure that the remote connection is adequately secured, by using tunneling and encryption protocols.
- Stop running vulnerable applications on the server, such as WebDAV. Unnecessary applications can be removed on a server by using Add/Remove Programs in the Windows Control Panel.
- Perform bound checking on input for web forms and query strings to prevent buffer overflow or malicious input attacks.
- Disable remote administration.
- Avoid printing error messages.
- Enable auditing and logging.
- Use a firewall between the web server and the Internet and allow only necessary ports (such as 80 and 443) through the firewall.
- Replace the GET method with the POST method when sending data to a web server

FOURTEEN
HACKING WEB APPLICATION

Web Application

A Web Application is a program that is accessed over a network connection using HTTP or HTTPS existing in the web server. The web application is a clientserver application which client run in web browser. The web application contains a set of web pages, scripts, images, etc. Web applications help organizations to grow their business.

Website

A website is a collection of web pages and related content that is identified by a common domain name and published on at least one web server. All publicly accessible websites collectively constitute the World Wide Web. Notable examples are wikipedia.org, google.com, and amazon.com. There are also private websites that can only be accessed on a private network, such as a company's internal website for its employees.

Websites are typically dedicated to a particular purpose, such as news, education, commerce, entertainment, or social networking. Hyperlinking between web pages guides the navigation of the site and starts with a home page. Users can access websites on a range of devices, including desktops, laptops, tablets, and smartphones. The software application used on these devices is called a web browser.

Types of websites

Static Website: A static website contains web pages with fixed content. A static site can be built using HTML and hosted on a Web server.

Dynamic Website: The information on dynamic website changes based on user interaction, the time zone, the viewer's native language, and other factors. These pages include Web scripting code, such as PHP or ASP. When a dynamic page is accessed, the code within the page is parsed on the Web server, and the resulting HTML is sent to the client web browser. Dynamic websites can interact with the user, capable of access information stored on the database. Dynamic web pages are also known as database-driven websites.

How A Web Application Works

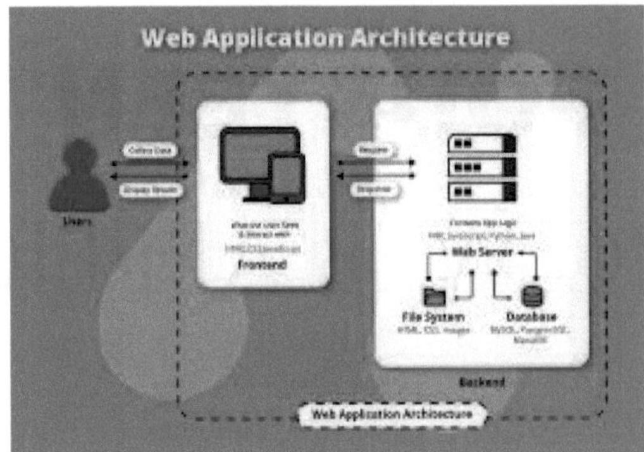

- The user sends a request to the web server over the internet through the web browser or the application interface in the form of URL or an HTML form
- Web server forward these requests to the web application server
- Web application server queries the database and generates the results for the requested task
- Web servers respond back to the client with the requested information.

OWASP

The Open Web Application Security Project (OWASP), an online community, produces freely-available articles, methodologies, documentation, tools, and technologies in the field of web application security. It aims to raise awareness about application security by identifying some of the most critical risks that organizations are facing.

OWASP Top 10 (2017 vs 2013):

- Injection (A1-2017 & A1-2013)
- Broken Authentication and Session Management (A2-2017 & A2-2013)
- Sensitive Data Exposure (A3-2017 & A6-2013)
- XXE - XML External Entities (New A4-2017)
- Broken Access Control (A5-2017)
- Insecure Direct Object Reference (A4-2013) and
- Missing Function level Access control (A7-2013)
- Security Misconfiguration (A6-2017 & A5-2013)
- XSS - Cross-Site Scripting (A7-2017& A3-2013)

- Insecure Deserialization (New A8-2017)
- Using Components with Known Vulnerabilities (A9-2017 & A9-2013)
- Insufficient Logging & Monitoring (New A10-2017)
- Cross-Site Request Forgery (A8-2013)
- Unvalidated Redirects and Forwards (A10-2013)

Parameter Tampering

This attack involves the manipulation of parameters exchanged between client and server to modify application data such as user credentials, permissions, price, the quantity of products. Establishing a proxy can make the process of tampering simple if the web application fails in proper session management.

Directory Traversal

- Directory Traversal or Path Traversal is an attack on HTTP which allows attackers to access restricted directories outside of the web server root location.
- Attackers try to access restricted directories that contain sensitive information like server configuration files, application source code, etc.
- Attackers can manage to access files located outside the web root because of this vulnerability.

Example: http://www.example.com/abc.php=../../../../etc/passwd

Cross-site scripting attack

- XSS attack takes advantage of dynamically generated web content based on user input provided on web pages.
- An attacker tries to inject commands in input fields provided on web pages.
- If the web server is unable to validate input fields on a web page properly, then it will execute the command provided by the attacker and unknowingly reveal information related to the client.

Types of XSS: Reflected XSS, Stored XSS, DOM Based XSS

Cross-site request forgery

Any request sent to the server are not validated (No server-side validation). The server processes the request without verifying whether the user made the request or not. Because of poor validation, requests can be forged and sent to users to force them to do things that they are not intended to do. By clicking some links, users may unknowingly change account passwords.

Command Injection

- Command injection vulnerability in a web application allows attackers to inject untrusted data and execute it as part of regular command or query.
- Attackers use specially crafted malicious commands or queries to exploit these vulnerabilities which may result in data loss.
- Injection attacks are possible because of poor web development capabilities.

File Inclusion

Local File Inclusion - Allows an attacker to gain access to any file on the server computer. An attacker can even access a file located apart from the web-root folder.

Remote File Inclusion - Allows an attacker to gain access to any file from any server. We can execute file located on a remote server on the vulnerable server.

Countermeasures

- Define access rights to private folders on the web server.
- Validate user input length, perform bound checking
- Use language-specific libraries for the programming language.
- Use the more secure HTTPS protocol instead of HTTP if available.
- Log out from online user accounts instead of directly closing the browser, to properly end sessions.
- Take careful note of security warnings from the web browser
- Avoid clicking links to sensitive portals, such as for e-banking, instead enter the URL of the website manually.
- Keep web application building software (frameworks) up to date to protect websites from application-based attacks

FIFTEEN
SQL INJECTION

SQL

SQL (Structured Query Language) is a database management language used to manage databases to perform various operations like create, read, update and delete on the database. SQL is used by database administrators, as well as developers to organize user data properly. Web applications interact with the database server in the form of queries. SQL queries include select, add, insert, update, delete, create, alter and truncate.

List of Database software

- MySQL
- Microsoft SQL
- Oracle
- MongoDB
- SQL lite
- Microsoft Access
- DB2 Express-C

Database

A database is a collection of information that is organized into rows, columns, and tables, and it is indexed so that it can be easily accessed, managed and updated. Data in the database gets updated, expanded and deleted as new information is added.

The relation between the Web server and Database server

A server is a software that runs continuously and responds to requests sent by the clients, Communication between a client and a server happens using a specific protocol example HTTP, HTTPS Server running web application include three components like

Web servers which primarily respond to HTTP / HTTPS requests sent by the clients and passes these requests on to handlers. **Application server** handles requests to create dynamic web pages. The application server processes the user request to generate the HTML page for the end user, instead of serving a static HTML page stored on the disk. Application server software runs on the same physical server machine as where the web server is running.

The database server is a server which houses a database application like JDBC, ODBC to provide database services to other computer programs. Most database applications respond to a query language. Each database understands its query language and converts each submitted query to server-readable form and executes it to retrieve results.

The relation between the web server and the database server are the web server uses the application server to retrieve the data from the database and host the data with the help of the web server application. So web server works as the front end, and database server works as a backend to provide data to web server.

SQL Injection

The technique used to take advantage of non-validated input vulnerabilities to pass SQL commands through a web application for execution on backend database to retrieve information directly from the database. It is used to gain unauthorized access to the database. SQL Injection is not a vulnerability in database or web server; it is a vulnerability in a web application which occurs due to lack of input validation.

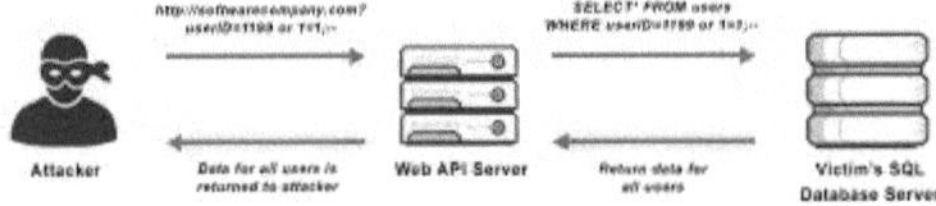

Types of SQL Injection attacks

- Authentication bypass attack
- Error-based SQL Injection
- Blind SQL Injection

Authentication bypass attack

The attacker uses this technique to bypass user authentication without providing the valid Username and password and tries to log into a web application with administrative privileges.

Error-based SQL Injection

Error-based SQL injection technique relies on error messages thrown by the database server to obtain information about the structure of the database. In some cases, error-based SQL injection alone is enough for an attacker to enumerate an entire database. While errors are very useful during the development phase of a web application, they should be disabled on a live site or logged to a file with restricted access instead. By analyzing these errors, the attacker can grab system information such as the database, database version, OS, etc.

Blind SQL injection

Blind SQL injection is a type of SQL Injection attack that queries the database true or false questions and determines the answer based on the applications response. This attack is often used when the web application is configured to show generic error messages but has not mitigated the code that is vulnerable to SQL injection. Blind SQL injection is nearly identical to normal SQL Injection, the only difference being the way the data is retrieved from the database.

Countermeasures

- Never trust user input. Sanitize and validate all input fields. Use parameterized statements, separate data from SQL code.
- Reject entries that contain binary data, escape sequences and comment characters.
- Checking the privileges of a user's connection to the database.
- Use secure hash algorithms to secure user passwords stored in the database.
- Perform source code review before hosting website.

SIXTEEN
WIFI HACKING

WiFi

- WiFi refers to wireless local area network (WLAN) works based on IEEE 802.11 standard. It is a widely used technology for wireless communication across a radio channel.
- Personal computers, smartphones, video game console, etc. use WiFi to connect to the internet via a wireless network access point.
- Every network card has a physical static address known as MAC address. This address is unique, and the card manufacturer assigns it.
- This address is used between devices to identify each other and to transfer packets to the right place. Each packet has a source MAC and a destination MAC.

WEP

Wired Equivalent Privacy (WEP) is a security algorithm for IEEE 802.11 wireless networks. Introduced as part of the original 802.11 standards ratified in 1997, its intention was to provide data confidentiality comparable to that of a traditional wired network. A Standard 64-bit WEP uses a 40-bit key (also known as WEP-40), which is concatenated with a 24-bit initialization vector (IV) to form the RC4 key used for encryption. RC4 is a stream cipher; the same traffic key must never be used twice. The purpose of an IV, which is transmitted as plain text, is to prevent any repetition, but a 24-bit IV is not long enough to ensure this on a busy network. The way the IV was used also opened WEP to a related key attack.

WPA

WPA stands for Wi-Fi Protected Access and is a security technology for Wi-Fi networks. It was developed in response to the weaknesses of WEP (Wired Equivalent Privacy) and therefore improves on WEP's authentication and encryption features.

WPA provides stronger encryption than WEP through use of either of two standard technologies: Temporal Key Integrity Protocol (TKIP) and Advanced Encryption Standard (AES). WPA also includes built-in authentication support that WEP does not offer. Some implementations of WPA allow for WEP clients to connect to the network too, but the security is then reduced to WEP-levels for all connected devices.

WPA includes support for authentication serves called Remote Authentication Dial-In User Service servers (RADIUS) servers. After connecting to a WPA network Once a device successfully connects to a WPA network. Devices make a four-way handshake with the access point to generate security keys.

When TKIP encryption is used, a message integrity code (MIC) is included to make sure that the data is not being spoofed. It replaces WEP's weaker packet guarantee called cyclic redundancy check (CRC).

WPA2

Short for Wi-Fi Protected Access 2, WPA2 is the security method added to WPA for wireless networks that provide stronger data protection and network access control. It provides enterprise and consumer Wi-Fi users with a high level of assurance that only authorized users can access their wireless networks. Based on the IEEE 802.11i standard, WPA2 provides government grade security by implementing the National Institute of Standards and Technology (NIST) FIPS 140-2 compliant AES encryption algorithm and 802.1x-based authentication.

There are two versions of WPA2: WPA2-Personal, and WPA2- Enterprise. WPA2-Personal protects unauthorized network access by utilizing a set-up password. WPA2-Enterprise verifies network users through a server. WPA2 is backward compatible with WPA.

WPA3

WPA3 is the next generation of Wi-Fi security and provides cutting-edge security protocols to the market. Building on the widespread success and adoption of Wi-Fi CERTIFIED WPA2™, WPA3 adds new features to simplify Wi-Fi security, enable more robust authentication, deliver increased cryptographic strength for highly sensitive data markets, and maintain resiliency of mission-critical networks. All WPA3 networks

- Use the latest security methods
- Disallow outdated legacy protocols
- Require use of Protected Management Frames (PMF)

Since Wi-Fi networks differ in usage purpose and security needs, WPA3 includes additional capabilities specifically for personal and enterprise networks. Users of WPA3-Personal receive increased protection from password guessing attempts, while WPA3-Enterprise users can now take advantage of higher grade security protocols for sensitive data networks.

WPA3 which retains interoperability with WPA2™ devices is currently an optional certification for Wi-Fi CERTIFIED devices. It will become required over time as market adoption grows.

WPA3-Personal

WPA3-Personal brings better protections to individual users by providing more robust password-based authentication, even when users choose passwords www.hackerschool.in that fall short of typical complexity recommendations. This capability is enabled through Simultaneous Authentication of Equals (SAE), which replaces Pre-shared Key (PSK) and WPA2-Personal. The technology is resistant to offline dictionary attacks where an adversary attempts to determine a network password by trying possible passwords without further network interaction.

- Natural password selection: Allows users to choose passwords that are easier to remember
- Ease of use: Delivers enhanced protections with no change to the way users connect to a network
- Forward secrecy: Protects data traffic even if a password is compromised after the data was transmitted

WPA3-Enterprise

WPA3-Enterprise. WPA3-Enterprise builds upon WPA2 and ensures the Enterprise, governments, and financial institutions have greater security with consistent application of security protocols across the network. WPA3-Enterprise also offers an optional mode using 192-bit minimum-strength security protocols and cryptographic tools to better protect sensitive data:

- Authenticated encryption: 256-bit Galois/Counter Mode Protocol (GCMP-256)
- Key derivation and confirmation: 384-bit Hashed Message Authentication Mode (HMAC) with Secure Hash Algorithm (HMACSHA384)
- Key establishment and authentication: Elliptic Curve Diffie-Hellman (ECDH) exchange and Elliptic Curve Digital Signature Algorithm (ECDSA) using a 384-bit elliptic curve
- Robust management frame protection: 256-bit Broadcast/Multicast Integrity Protocol Galois Message Authentication Code (BIP-GMAC256)

The 192-bit security mode offered by WPA3-Enterprise ensures the right combination of cryptographic tools are used and sets a consistent baseline of security within a WPA3 network.

Types of Wireless AntennasDirectional Antenna is used to broadcast and obtain radio waves from a single direction.

Omnidirectional Antenna provides a 360-degree horizontal radiation pattern. It is used in wireless base stations.

Parabolic Grid Antenna is based on the principle of a satellite dish, but it does not have a solid backing. They can pick up WiFi signals ten miles or more.

Yagi Antenna is a unidirectional antenna commonly used in communications for a frequency band of 10 MHz to VHF and UHF.

Dipole Antenna is a bidirectional antenna, used to support client connections rather than site-to-site applications.

Finding Open WiFi Networks

War Walking - Attackers walk around with WiFi-enabled laptops to detect open wireless networks.

War Chalking - A method used to draw symbols in public places to advertise open WiFi networks.

War Flying - In this technique, attackers use drones to detect open wireless networks.

War Driving - Attackers drive around with WiFi-enabled laptops to detect open wireless networks.

Aircrack-ng

Aircrack-ng includes a set of tools to perform WiFi network hacking.

Monitoring: Packet capture and export of data to text files for further processing by third-party tools.

Attacking: Replay attacks, deauthentication, fake access points and others via packet injection.

Testing: Checking WiFi cards and driver capabilities (capture and injection).

Cracking: WEP and WPA PSK (WPA 1 and 2).

Airmon-ng

This script can be used to enable monitor mode on wireless interfaces. It may also be used to go back from monitor mode to managed mode. Entering the airmon-ng command without parameters will show the interfaces status.

Airodump-ng

Airodump-ng is used for packet capturing of raw 802.11 frames and is particularly suitable for collecting WEP IVs (Initialization Vector) for the intent of using them with aircrack-ng. If you have a GPS receiver connected to the computer, airodump-ng is capable of logging the coordinates of the found access points. Additionally, airodump-ng writes out several files containing the details of all access points and clients seen.

Terminology

Bssid = Mac Address of The Access Point

Essid = Name of The Access Point

Ch = Channel Number of Access Point

Data = Data Packets Transferred

Beacons = Advertisement Packets Sent by Access Point

Pwr = Signal Strength of Access Point

Auth = Encryption Used by The Access Point

Cipher = Encryption Cipher Used by The Access Point

Aireplay-ng

Aireplay-ng is used to inject frames. The primary function is to generate traffic for the later use in aircrack-ng for cracking the WEP and WPA-PSK keys. There are different attacks which can cause de-authentications to capture WPA handshake data, fake authentications, Interactive packet replay, handcrafted ARP request injection and ARP-request reinjection. With the packet forge-ng tool, it's possible to create arbitrary frames. Most drivers need to be patched to be able to inject,

Airbase-ng

Airbase-ng is a multi-purpose tool aimed at attacking clients as opposed to the Access Point (AP) itself. Since it is so versatile and flexible, summarizing it is a challenge. Here are some of the feature highlights:

- Implements the Caffe Latte WEP client attack
- Implements the Hirte WEP client attack
- Ability to cause the WPA/WPA2 handshake to be captured
- Ability to act as an ad-hoc Access Point
- Ability to serve as a full Access Point
- Ability to filter by SSID or client MAC addresses
- Ability to manipulate and resend packets
- Ability to encrypt sent packets and decrypt received packets

WEP Cracking

It uses a stream cipher algorithm called RC4 where each packet is encrypted at the AP and is then decrypted at the client, WEP ensures that each packet has a unique keystream by using a random 24-bit Initialization Vector (IV), this IV is contained in the packets as plain text.

In a busy network we can collect more than two packets with the same IV, then we can use the aircrack-ng suite to determine WEP key.

Cracking WPA/WPA2 Encryption

Capturing WPA packets is not useful as they do not contain any info that can be used to crack the key. The only packet that contains info that helps us crack the password is the handshake packets.

Every time a client connects to that AP a four-way handshake occurs between the client and the AP. By capturing the handshake, we can use aircrack to launch a word list attack against the handshake to determine the key.

To crack a WPA/WPA2 AP with WPS disabled, we need two things:

1. Capture the Handshake
2. A wordlist

Cracking the WPA Key using a wordlist

Use aircrack-ng to crack the key. It performs the job by combining each password in the wordlist with AP names (Essid) to compute a PMK (Pairwise Master Key) using the pbkdf2 algorithm; the PMK is then compared to the handshake file. Create wordlist using crunch tool to crack the WPA key

Exploiting WPS Feature

WPS is a feature that allows users to connect to WPS enabled networks easily, using a WPS button or only by clicking on WPS functionality. Authentication is done using an eight-digit long pin, this means that there is a relatively small number of pin combination and using brute force we can guess the pin in less than 10 hours. Tools like wifite or reaver can automate this process and recover the WPA key from that pin.

Note: This flaw is in the WPS feature and not in WPA/WPA2. However, it allows us to crack any WPA/WPA2 AP without using a wordlist and without any clients. Cracking WiFi Passwords (Summary)

Bluetooth hacking: Attackers take advantage of Bluetooth to perform various types of attacks. They exploit vulnerabilities in Bluetooth stack implementation to gain access to sensitive data in Bluetooth enabled devices and networks. Attackers gain sensitive information by hacking a Bluetooth enabled device from another Bluetooth enabled device.

Bluetooth attacks - Btlejacking, Bluesmacking, Bluejacking, Bluesnarfing, Bluesniff, and Blueprinting.

Countermeasures

- Do not use WEP encryption, as it is easy to crack.
- Use WPA2 with a complex password, make sure the password contains small letters, capital letters, symbols and numbers
- Ensure that the WPS feature is disabled as it can be used to crack your complex WPA2 key by brute-forcing the easy WPS pin.
- Enable MAC address filtering on access point or router.
- Set default router access password and enable firewall protection.

SEVENTEEN

HACKING MOBILE PLATFORMS

Mobile operating system

A mobile operating system is an OS that is specifically designed to run on mobile devices such as mobile phones, smartphones, PDAs, tablet computers and other handheld devices. Mobile operating systems combine features of a personal computer operating system with other features useful for mobile or handheld use

List of Mobile OS

1. Android OS
2. Bada
3. BlackBerry OS
4. iPhone OS / iOS
5. Palm OS
6. Symbian OS
7. webOS
8. Windows Mobile

Terms in Mobile Hacking

Stock ROM: It is the default ROM (operating system) of an Android Device.

Rooting: Rooting is the process of allowing users of smartphones, tablets and other devices running the Android mobile operating system to attain privileged control (known as root access) over various Android subsystems.

Lineage OS: LineageOS is a free and open-source operating system for smartphones and tablet computers, based on the Android mobile platform. It is the successor to the custom ROM Cyanogen Mod

Bricking Mobile: A device that does not turn on and function normally. The bricked device cannot be fixed through normal procedures. Devices are bricked due to overwriting of the Firmware or low-level system software.

Bring Your Own Device (BYOD): Bring your own device (BYOD) is a business policy that allows employees to bring their mobile devices to their workplace.

Mobile Platform Vulnerabilities and Risks

- Malicious Apps in Store
- Mobile Malware
- Jailbreaking or Rooting
- Mobile Application Vulnerabilities
- Weak Data Security and App Encryption
- Excessive Permissions
- Weak Communication Security

Android OS

Android is a mobile operating system developed by Google, based on a modified version of the Linux kernel and other open source software and designed primarily for touchscreen mobile devices such as smartphones and tablets.

Android Architecture

Android Architecture is implemented in the form of a software stack architecture consisting of a Linux kernel, a runtime environment and corresponding libraries, an application framework and a set of applications.

iPhone OS (IOS)

iOS is a mobile operating system created and developed by Apple Inc. and distributed exclusively for Apple hardware. It is a proprietary operating system which runs on Apple mobile devices (iPhone, iPad, and iPod touch).

iOS Architecture

The architecture of iOS is a layered architecture. At the uppermost level iOS works as an intermediary between the underlying hardware and the applications running on the device. Apps communicate with the hardware through a collection of well-defined system interfaces instead of directly interacting with hardware. Interfaces make it simple to write apps that constantly work on devices having various hardware abilities.

Hacking Android Device

- Hacking Android By using Malicious App Infection

1. Dendroid
2. Droid Jack
3. AndroRAT

- Using Kernel Level Vulnerabilities to Exploit Mobile Devices

1. Stage Fright

General Guidelines for Mobile Security

- Do not load too many applications and avoid auto-upload of photos to social networks.
- Securely wipe or delete the data disposing of the device.
- Turn of Bluetooth if it is not necessary.
- Do not share the information within GPS-enabled apps unless they are necessary.
- Install applications from trusted application stores.

Countermeasures

- Do not directly download Android Package Files from untrusted websites.
- Never root your Android device.
- Update the operating system regularly.
- Use iOS devices on a secured and protected WiFi network.
- Deploy only trusted third-party applications on iOS devices.
- Configure 'Find My iPhone' and utilize it to wipe a lost or stolen device.
- In the case of IT companies, it is important to educate employees in the organization about the BYOD policy.

EIGHTEEN

IoT (Internet of Things)

IoT (Internet of Things)

Internet of Things is the concept of connecting any device to the Internet and to other connected devices, which collect and share data about the way they are designated. The 'thing' in IoT could be a person with a heart monitor or an automobile with built-in-sensors, i.e., objects can collect and transfer data over a network without manual assistance or intervention. The technology, i.e., embedded in the objects help them to interact with other devices and sensors.

The information collected by different devices can be used to detect patterns, make recommendations, and detect possible problems before they occur. The data collected by connected devices enable smart decision making based on real-time information, which helps users to save time and money.

The IoT devices are often divided into consumer, enterprise, and infrastructure spaces based on the functions. The examples of IoT devices are

- Smart Thermostat.
- Switch Smart Plug.
- Smart Bulbs.
- Smart Lock.
- Smart Security System.
- SmartThings Hub
- Smart Pet Feeder.
- Smart Health Monitor
- Car Tracking Adapter
- IoT Tracking and Monitoring

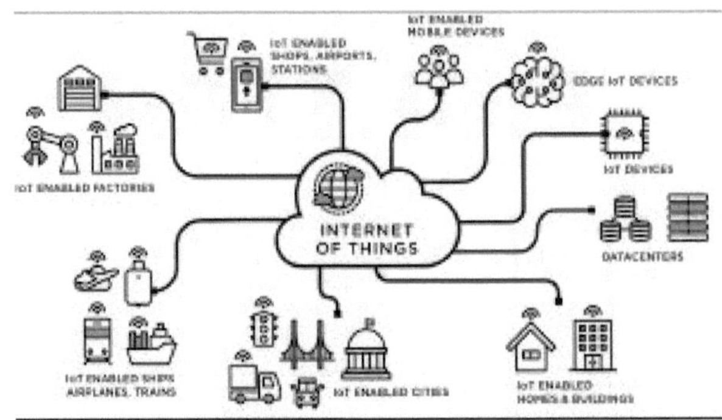

IoT Vulnerabilities

- **Insecure Web Interface:** It can result in data loss, lack of accountability, denial of access and can lead to complete device takeover.
- **Insufficient Authentication/Authorization:** It can result in complete compromise of the device and user accounts.
- **Insecure Network Services:** It can result in the facilitation of attacks on other devices.
- **Lack of Transport Encryption/Integrity Verification:** It can result in data expose, and could open doors to compromise the device or user accounts.
- **Privacy Concerns:** Collecting personal data and storing it without applying any protection can lead to the identity theft.
- **Insecure Cloud Interface:** It could cause a threat to user data which can be used to take control of the device.
- **Insecure Mobile Interface:** It can be easy to discover by simply reviewing the connection to the wireless networks and by using the password reset mechanism to identify valid accounts which can lead to account enumeration.
- **Insufficient security configurability:** It could lead to compromise of the device whether intentional or accidental.
- **Insecure Software/Firmware:** Capturing update files via unencrypted connections, the update file itself is not encrypted, or they can perform their malicious update via DNS hijacking. The attack could come from the local network or the internet.
- **Poor Physical Security:** Using vectors such as USB ports, SD cards or other storage means to access the Operating System and potentially any data stored on the device.

OT (Operational Technology):

Operational Technology is a combination of software and hardware designed to detect or cause changes in industrial operations. OT systems are used in various industries like Manufacturing, Mining, Healthcare, Defence,

Transportation to ensure the safety of physical devices and their operations in the network. Any system that analyses and processes operational data which includes devices like switches, lights, sensors, robots, surveillance cameras can be part of OT. Older versions of software and hardware make OT systems vulnerable for cyber-attacks. Attackers can take full control of vulnerable OT systems to steal critical business or operational data. It is also possible to shut down the plant or block the production by performing DoS attacks.

IoT Device Hacking

The objective is to compromise smart devices like automobiles, printers, door locks, washing machines, etc., to gain unauthorized access to network resources and IoT devices. By hacking IoT devices, a hacker can gain following benefit:

- Create a botnet of the compromised IoT devices to launch DDoS attacks.
- Sell compromised data in black markets.
- Carry out malicious activities on compromised IoT devices.
- Install ransomware to block access to an IoT device and demand for ransom.
- Compromised IoT device could be used to steal the identity of a victim and carry out credit card related frauds.
- Compromised smart cameras could be used to snoop on families.

Attacks on IoT devices

- DDoS attack.
- The attack on HVAC systems.
- Rolling code attack.
- Blue borne attack.
- Jamming attack.
- Remote access using the backdoor.
- Remote access using telnet
- Man in the middle attack.

Countermeasures

- Default configurations should be changed during the initial setup.
- Password recovery mechanisms must be robust.
- Ensure that user credentials are properly protected.
- Implement two-factor authentications to guard against unauthorized access.
- Make sure that only the necessary ports are exposed and available.

- Ensure that services are not vulnerable to DoS or buffer overflow attacks.
- Use secure protocols such as SSL and TLS while transiting data over the network.
- Make sure that cloud-based web interface is not susceptible for XSS, SQL Injection or CSRF attacks
- Services should have the ability to separate regular users from users with administrative privileges.
- All smart devices must be updated on a regular base.

NINETEEN
CLOUD COMPUTING

Cloud Computing

Cloud Computing is the practice of using a network of remote servers hosted on the internet to store, manage, and process data, rather than a local server or a personal computer. The information being accessed is found in "the cloud" so the user need not to be in a specific place to gain access in which data is stored.

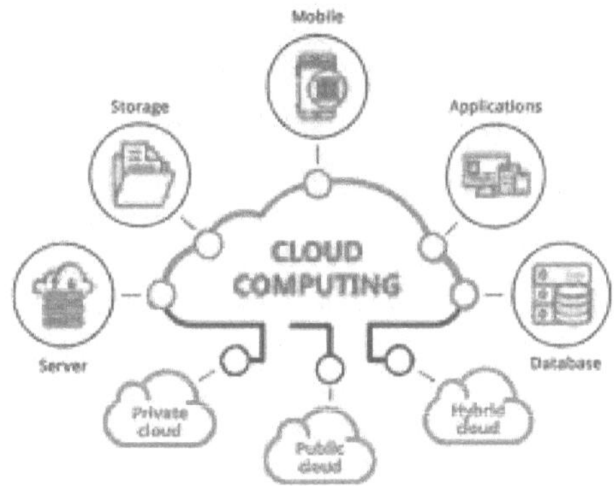

cloud computing

Characteristics of cloud computing

- On-demand self-service
- Distributed storage
- Rapid elasticity

- Automated management
- Broad network access
- Resource pooling
- Measured service
- Virtualization technology
- Pay per use

Cloud Computing Services

1. Infrastructure as a Service (IaaS)
2. Platform as a service (PaaS)
3. Software as a service (SaaS)

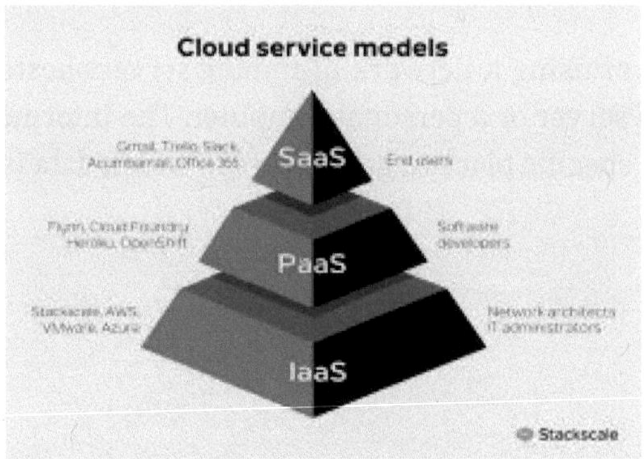

Infrastructure as a Service (IaaS)

Infrastructure-as-a-Service (IaaS) provides virtual machines and other abstracted hardware and operating systems which may be controlled through service API. In these services, cloud service providers install operating system images, and application software's on the cloud infrastructure based on user's requirement. The cloud service provider is responsible for patching and maintains the operating systems and the application software.

Examples: Amazon EC2, SkyDrive, etc.

Platform-as-a-Service (PaaS)

Platform-as-a-Service (PaaS) offers development tools, configuration management, and development platforms on-demand that can be used by subscribers to develop custom applications; typically it includes a framework that satisfies the requirement of a developer. The Application developers can take advantage of using the licensed software without worrying about the cost and complexity involved in maintaining the underlying hardware and software layers.

Examples: Google App Engine, Microsoft Azure, etc.

Software as a Service (SaaS)

Software-as-a-Service (SaaS) offers software to subscribers on-demand over the Internet. CSP (Cloud service provider) manages the infrastructure and platforms that run these applications. This service eliminates the need for installing and running the applications on the user's computers.

Examples: Google Docs, Calendar, Web-based office applications, etc.

Cloud deployment models

- Public cloud
- Private cloud
- Community cloud
- Hybrid Cloud

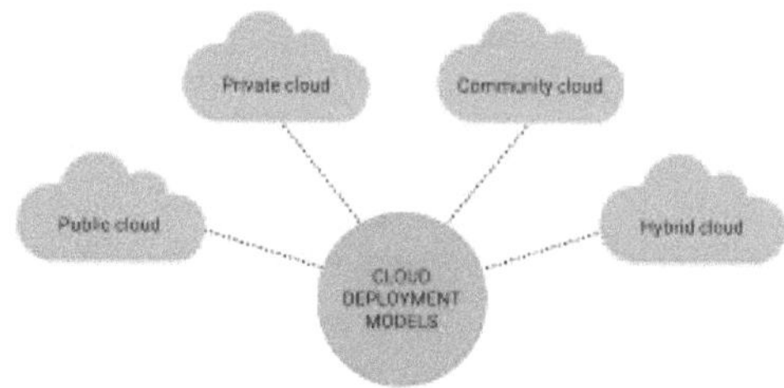

Public cloud

In the public cloud model, the cloud service provider delivers the cloud service over the internet to users. Where users no need to worry about the infrastructure. The cost is shared by all users, for free or in the form of a license policy like pay per user.

Private Cloud

Private Cloud infrastructure is operated solely by a single organization. The services are delivered from an organizational data center to internal users of the organization. This model preserves the management, control, and security to organizational data centers. Internal users may not be billed for services. Private clouds are great for organizations that have high-security demands, high management demands and uptime requirements.

Community cloud

Community Cloud infrastructure is mutually shared between organizations that belong to a specific community with common concerns (security, compliance, etc.). The community members generally share similar privacy, performance and security concerns. A community cloud can be managed by hosting it internally or by a third-party provider. A community cloud is good for organizations that work on joint ventures that need centralized cloud computing ability for managing, building and executing their projects. The best example for community cloud is a cloud for the bank or trading firm.

Hybrid Cloud

Hybrid cloud computing uses a combination of two or more cloud deployment models, like private cloud and public cloud services. This service allows workloads to be shared between private and public clouds. Companies can run mission-critical workloads or sensitive applications on the private cloud and use the public cloud to handle workload bursts or spikes in demand. An organization can use the public cloud to interact with their customers while keeping their data secured through a private cloud.

Cloud Computing Benefits:

Economic

- Environment-friendly
- Less maintenance
- Less power consumption

Operational

- Deploy applications quickly
- Scale as needed

Staffing

- Less IT staffs
- Well usage of resources
- Less personnel training

Security

- Less investment in security
- Better disaster recovery
- Effective patch management and implementation of security updates

Cloud Computing Threats

- Illegal access to the Cloud
- Privilege Escalation.
- Hardware Failure.
- VM-Level attacks.
- Cryptanalysis Attacks.
- SQL Injection Attacks.
- DoS and DDoS Attacks.
- Session Hijacking using XSS Attacks.
- Loss of Business Reputation due to Co-tenant Activity

Container technology:

A Container is a package of an application or software including all its dependencies such as library files, configuration files, binaries and other resources that run independently in the cloud environment.

Containers-as-a-Service (CaaS) is a service model of cloud computing that lets users deploy and manage applications through container-based abstraction using on-premises data centres or the cloud. This includes virtualization and management of containers through orchestrators. CaaS is useful to developers in building scalable containerized apps that are more secure. Amazon AWS EC2, Docker, Kubernetes are popular container services.

Serverless computing:

Serverless computing also known as FaaS (Function-as-a-Service) simplifies the process of application deployment and eliminates the need for managing the server and hardware by the developers.

Countermeasures

- Enforce data protection, backup and retention mechanisms.
- Disclose relevant logs and data to customers.
- Prevent unauthorized server access using security checkpoint.
- Monitor the client's traffic for any malicious activity.
- Implement strong key generation, stronger authentication management, and destruction practices.
- Check for data protection at both design and runtime.
- Enforce legal contracts in employee behavior policy.
- Prohibit users from sharing application and services credentials.
- Ensure that physical security is a 24 x 7
- Leverage strong two-factor authentication techniques where possible

TWENTY

CRYPTOGRAPHY

Cryptography

Cryptography is a process of converting plain text data (readable) into ciphertext (unreadable) data to protect confidentiality so that unauthorized users cannot understand what is transmitted. Encryption algorithms are used to perform mathematical computation on data using the key and convert data to ciphertext. The algorithm that is chosen to perform encryption with some key can also be used for decryption. Decryption is the process of converting ciphertext to plaintext. Encryption is a reversible operation, i.e., converting plaintext to ciphertext and vice versa is possible using the algorithm and key. Cryptography is used to protect the confidentiality of information shared on the internet such as email messages, chat sessions, web transactions, personal data, corporate data, e-commerce applications, etc.

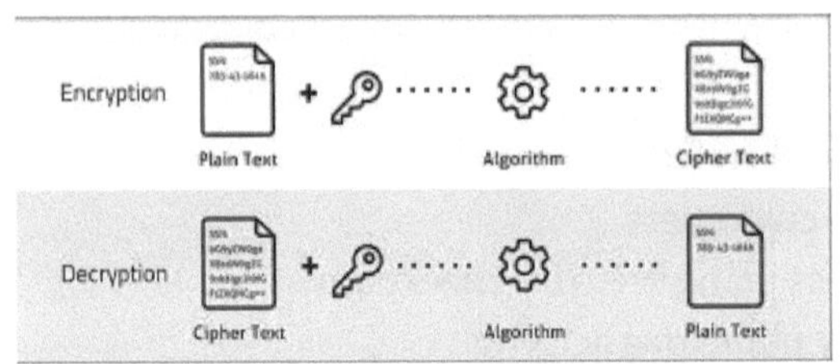

Objectives of Cryptography

Confidentiality: To ensure that private or confidential information is not made available or disclosed to unauthorized individuals.

Integrity: To ensure that an unauthorized individual does not tamper the information exchanged over the internet.

Availability: To ensure that services are not denied to authorized users.

Types of Cryptography

Based on the number of keys used for encryption they are classified into two types

- Symmetric key cryptography
- Asymmetric key cryptography

Symmetric Encryption

The symmetric key algorithm is also known as the secret key algorithm. Symmetric key algorithms use the same cryptographic key for both encryption and decryption. Data Encryption Standard (DES) and Advanced Encryption Standard (AES) algorithms are the most commonly used symmetric key algorithm which uses a key at sender side for encryption, and the receiver uses the same key for decryption. To make two parties (sender and receiver) to communicate confidentially, they must first exchange the secret key so that each party can encrypt messages to send and decrypt messages to read. This process is known as key exchange. This key is shared between two parties over a secure channel. Based on input data these algorithms can be further divided into two categories

Block ciphers: Block ciphers encrypt data one block at a time.

Stream ciphers: Stream ciphers encrypt data byte by byte.

The strength of any cryptographic algorithm depends on the secrecy of the key. If keys are not securely shared, then unauthorized parties can gain access to a secret key used for encryption and they can un-encrypt data and read every packet shared between two parties.

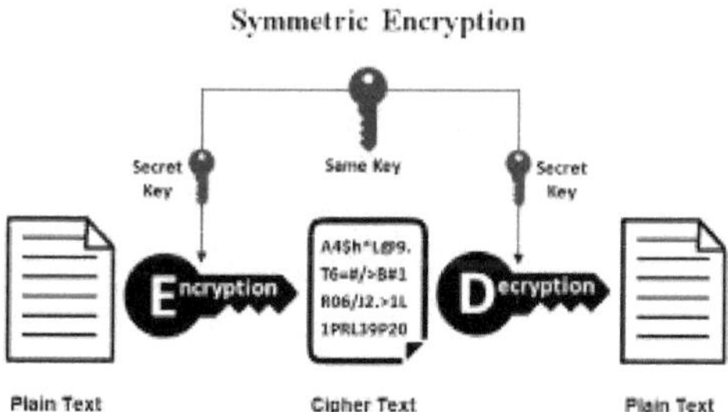

Asymmetric Encryption

Asymmetric key algorithms use two different keys known as a public key and a private key for encryption and decryption. The sender and receiver generate a private key which is kept secret (not shared with anyone) and a public key which is shared with other parties. In case of asymmetric algorithms, senders encrypt messages using the receiver's public key. The receiver's private key can only decrypt this encrypted message. In this manner, it ensures that both the confidentiality and integrity of information are preserved. The best part of asymmetric encryption is its Key Management system; it takes advantage of Public Key Infrastructure for proper management of public keys.

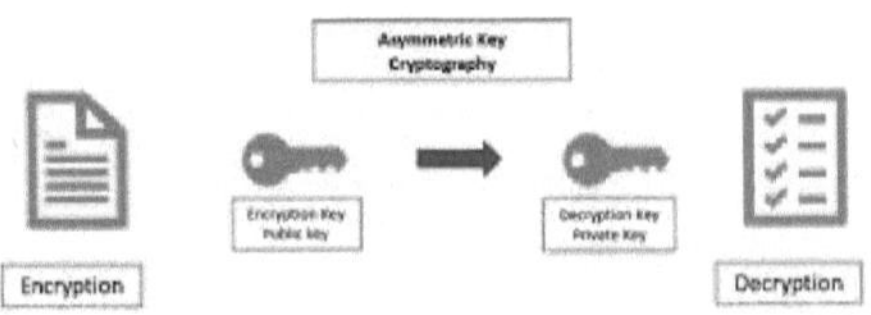

Cipher

In cryptography, a cipher is an algorithm that performs encryption or decryption in a series of well-defined steps that can be followed as a procedure. Ciphers are classified based on input data, a number of keys used for encryption.

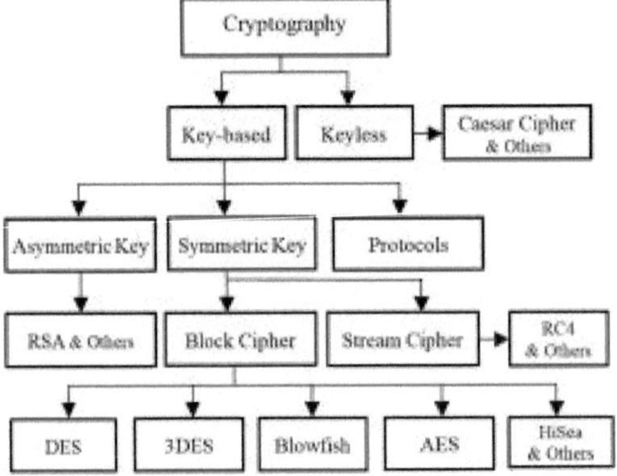

Classical ciphers

Classical ciphers are cryptographic algorithms that have been used in the past (practically computed and solved manually). Classical ciphers are often divided into substitution ciphers and transposition ciphers.

Substitution cipher: In a substitution cipher, letters are systematically replaced throughout the message for other letters. In these cipher method monoalphabetic substitution ciphers, where just one cipher alphabet is used. Polyalphabetic substitution cipher, where multiple cipher alphabets are used.

Transposition ciphers: In a transposition cipher, the letters themselves are kept unchanged, but their order within the message is scrambled. Many transposition ciphers are done according to geometric design.

Modern ciphers

Modern ciphers are designed based on various concepts of mathematics such as number theory, computational complexity theory, and probability theory. It needs the computational power to encrypt and decrypt the data. Modern encryption methods are divided into two type based on input data (Block and Stream ciphers), and a number of keys (secret key and public key) used.

Hash function

A hash function performs a series of mathematical operations to convert input data into a fixed length alphanumeric characters. The input to the hash function is an arbitrary length, but the output is always of fixed length.

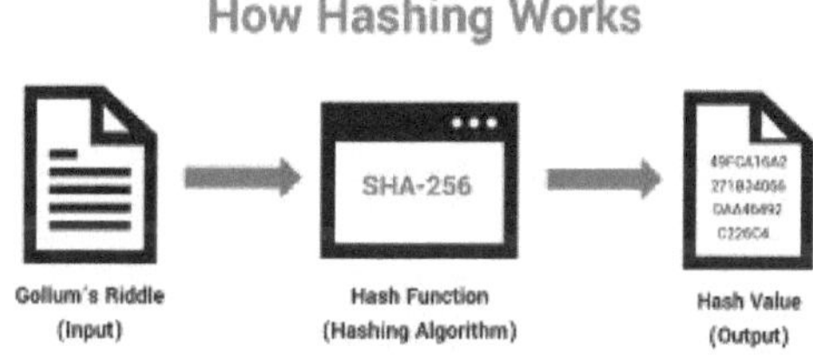

Features of Hash Functions

- Fixed Length Output: Hash function converts data of arbitrary length to a fixed length.
- The efficiency of Operation: Computationally hash functions are much faster than asymmetric encryption.

Examples of the Hash functions These are examples of well-known hash functions:

Hashed Message Authentication Code (HMAC): Combines authentication via a shared secret with hashing.

Message Digest 2 (MD2): Byte-oriented, produces a 128-bit hash value from an arbitrary-length message, designed for smart cards.

MD4: Similar to MD2, designed specifically for fast processing in software.

MD5: Similar to MD4 but slower because the data is manipulated more.

Secure Hash Algorithm (SHA): Modeled after MD4 and proposed by NIST for the Secure Hash Standard (SHS), produces a 160-bit hash value.

Steganography

Steganography is an art of hiding a secret message within an ordinary message and extracting it at the destination to maintain the confidentiality of data. The program named 'snow' is used to conceal messages in ASCII text by appending whitespace to the end of lines. There are different tools that can hide text in pictures so that to retrieve the hidden secret message the receiver must use the same tool as sender used to hide the text message. Steganalysis is the art of discovering and rendering secret messages using steganography.

Cryptography Attacks

Cryptography attacks are based on the assumption that the cryptanalyst has access to the encrypted information.

- Chosen plaintext
- Adaptive chosen plaintext attack
- Known plaintext
- Known ciphertext
- Chosen ciphertext
- Chosen key
- Rubber cosh cryptanalysis

Brute force attack is a process of defeating a cryptographic scheme by trying a large number of possible keys until the correct encryption key is discovered.

TWENTY-ONE
TIPS

BUG BOUNTY

1. LEARN COMPUTER NETWORKING

A DECENT KNOWLEDGE OF COMPUTER NETWORKS IS VERY MUCH NECESSARY FOR GETTING STARTED WITH THE BUG BOUNTY.

LEARN INTERNET,HTTP,TCP/IP,OSI,ETC.

2. GET FEMILIZED WITH THE WEB TECHNOLOGIES

THIS INCLUDES GETTING A BASIC UNDERSTANDING OF WEB PROGRAMMING AND WEB PROTOCOLS.

WEB TECHNOLOGIES ,JAVA- SCRIPT,PHP.

3. LEARN LINUX & COMMAND LINE

IN LINUX YOU NEED TO UNDERSTAND FROM THE BASICS OF THE ADVANCED LEARN THE CONSOLE COMMANDS AND HOW TO NAVIGATE AND DO EVERYTHING FROM YOUR CONSOLE.

4. OWASP TOP 10

THE OWASP TOP 10 PROVIDES RANKING AND REMEDIATION GUIDANCE FOR THE TOP 10 MOST CRITICAL WEB APPLICATION SECURITY RISKS.

5. CHOOSE YOUR PATH

WEB PENETRATION TESTING

ANDROID APPLICATION PENTESTING

IOS APPLICATION PENTESTING

PHASES OF PENETRATION TESTING

1. INFO GATHERING

2. RECONNAISSANCE
3. DISCOVERY & SCANNING
4. VULNERABILITY ASSESSMENT
5. EXPLOITATION
6. FINAL EXPLOITATION & REVIEW
7. UTILIZE THE TESTING RESULTS

TOP BEST TOOLS FOR OSINT

OSINT FRAMEWORK
METASPLOIT
SPIDERFOOT
SHODAN
NMAP
MALTEGO
THE HARVESTER
ZOOMEYE
GOOGLE DORKS

HOW DO HACKERS HACK SERVERS

- THERE ARE TWO PRIMARY WAYS A SERVER MAY BE COMPROMISED.
- THE HACKER HAS GUESSED THE PASSWORD OFA USER ON THE SERVER. THE HACKER HAS GUESSED A PASSWORD OF A USER ON THE SERVER
- THE HACKER HAS GAINED ACCESS THROUGH A SECURITY HOLE IN A WEB APPLICATION SUCH AS WORDPRESS, JOOMLA DRUPAL, ETC.
- HACKERS CAN REMOTELY SCAN SERVERS TO DETERMINE VULNERABILITIES WITHIN THAT SYSTEM.
- ONCE THEY FIND A VULNERABILITY, THEY EXPLOIT IT BY SENDING A COMMAND OR DATA TO THE SERVER THAT WILL CAUSE THE APPLICATION TO CRASH AND WILL THEN START EXECUTING CODE.

NETWORKING DEVICES YOU MUST KNOW

1. **REPEATER**

A repeater regenerate the signal over the same network

Note- they do not amplify the signal but copy the signal bit by bit and regenerate it at the original strength.

2. **HUB**

A hub is basically a multiport repeater.

it is a dumb device, ie hubs can not filter data, so data packets are sent to all connected devices and can't find the best path for data transfer.

There are three types of hubs

Active Hub: These are the hubs that have their own power supply and can clean, boost and relay the signal along with the network.

passive Hub: these are the hubs that collect writing from nodes and power supply from the active hub

intelligent Hub: it works like active hub and includes remote management capabilities.

4. Bridge

A bridge operates at the data link layer

A bridge has functionality of filtering content by reading the MAC addresses of source and destination

it is also used for interconnecting two LANs working on the same protocol.

There are two types of bridges

Transparent Bridges:- These are the bridge in which the station are completely unaware of the bridges existence

Source Routing Bridges:- in these bridges, routing operation is performed by the source station and the frame specifies which route to follow.

ÞÞÞ

TEMPORARY EMAIL SERVICES

1. EMAILONDECK
2. 10MINUTEMAIL
3. MAILINATOR
4. E4WARD
5. TEMPMAIL
6. GUERRILLA MAIL
7. THROWAWAYE MAIL
8. GETNADA
9. YOPMAIL

ÞÞÞ

GITHUB REPO FOR HACKERS

- H@*KER ROADMAP
- AWESOME-H@CKING
- PENTESTING-BIBLE
- PAYLOADSALL THETHINGS
- H@CKING-SECURITY-EBOOKS
- CHEATSHEET-GOD
- NAHAMSEC
- EDOVERFLOW

WEBSITES TO TEST YOUR HACKING SKILLS

1. PWNABLE.KR
2. CTFLEARN.COM
3. ROOT-ME.ORG
4. CRACKMES.ONE
5. PANTEST.TRAINING
6. MICROCORRUPTION.COM
7. TRYHACKME.COM
8. HACKING-LAB.COM
9. GAMEOFHACKS.COM

TOP5 HACKING TOOLS

- BURPSUITE
- METASPOLIT
- ACUNETIX
- NMAP
- WIRESHARK

INFORMATION GATHERING TOOLS

- NMAP
- RECON-NG
- AMASS
- OSINT
- MALTEGO

WHERE CAN I PRACTICE HACKING

1. PORTSWIGGER'S WEB SECURITY ACADEMY LABS
2. HACKTHEBOX
3. HACKTHISSITE
4. PENTESTERLAB
5. HELLBOUND HACKERS

TOP 5 HACKING GADGETS

- RASPBERRY -PI
- WIFI KILLER
- KEY LOGGER
- USB RUBBER DUCKEY
- USB KILLER

TO LEARN ANYTHING FREE VIST:<<< www.freelearninglist.org >>>

CAREER PATHS FOR AN ETHICAL HACKER

1. PENETRATION TESTER
2. DATA SECURITY ANALYST
3. NETWORK ADMINISTRATOR
4. WEB SECURITY ADMINISTRATOR
5. DIGITAL FORENSICS INVESTIGATOR

🏳🏳🏳

6 BEST PLATFORMS FOR BUG BOUNTY

- HACKERONE
- BUGCROWD
- SYNACK
- YESWEHACK
- HACKENPROOF
- INTIGRITI

🏳🏳🏳

6 BEST FREE VPN SERVICES

- PROTONVPN
- WINDSCRIBE
- TUNNELBEAR
- HOTSPOT SHIELD
- SPEEDIFY
- HIDE.ME

🏳🏳🏳

FOR ANY INFORMATION REFER MEDIUM ACCOUNT@CYBERFLASH

🏳🏳🏳

Printed by Libri Plureos GmbH in Hamburg,
Germany